UNEARTHING
A
SERIAL KILLER

David Paul and Kevin F. McMurray

David Paul
108 Village Square, Unit 158
Somers, NY 10589
dpaul@unearthingaserialkiller.com

Notes

CONTENTS

ACKNOWLEDGMENTS

This book would not have been possible without the cooperation of the Mattina Family. Their remarkable courage and ongoing commitment to find the truth about the crimes perpetrated against their precious Antonella; is as strong today as it was on that July day in 1984.

Much thanks to Tom McGurn, who though just days into his much deserved retirement, made good on a promise, to provide information in regards to his late friend, Gary Stymiloski and his beliefs about Alex J. Mengel. Tom was always available to take a phone call or respond to the myriad of e-mails and texts. He provided keen insight and many key contacts for our research.

Mike DeRosa was one of those contacts. Mike's candor and contributions to this project cannot be overstated. His investigative skill and the passion shown in his pursuit to bring justice to a fallen brother officer, should be a required block of instruction, at Police Academies across the country.

Thanks to the iconic Mary Murphy, for recognizing the importance of this story and her outstanding segment on it.

A special thanks to Sgt. Anthony Morizio of the WCDPS for providing hundreds of FOIA documents and materials in an always timely manner.

— David Paul and Kevin F. McMurray
    September 2, 2015.

"A civilized society should not accept that children simply disappear" …

— John Mallon,
Flushing, Queens

1

1985
Catskills Region
East Durham, New York

A chill came over New Jersey Search and Rescue Dog Handler Robert Langendoen on this Ides of March afternoon. He was certain now that he and his beloved scent dog, Flash, had located the "package" they sought after searching the heavily-wooded area for nearly five hours.

Langendoen and Flash, a pure white German shepherd, were one of two teams that responded from the nationally renowned all-volunteer organization to the unincorporated village in the Town of Durham, following an urgent request the night before from the New York State Police.

The Village of East Durham is a two hour drive north of Manhattan and has a population of just 2,500. Known for its vast Irish Culture and burgeoning week-long summer festivals, the village long ago secured the title *Irish Village USA*.

Kidnapping, murder, and international manhunts were as foreign to this village as a San Gennaro Feast.

Langendoen and Flash's find proved to be the lynchpin in ensuring that a self-confessed cop killer would also answer for the murder of his only other known victim. A murder so heinous that, years later, art may very well have imitated life, namely in the 1991 Oscar-winning film, *The Silence of the Lambs*.

2

In 1985, the affluent County of Westchester, New York's Department of Public Safety arrived on the law enforcement landscape as a formidable policing agency. For the suburban community that was contiguous with the greatest city in the world, police excellence was vitally important.

At best, the path had been contentious, rife with political battles and back room deals. The most controversial aspect of all was the 1979 merger of the parkway police and sheriff's department into the Westchester County Department of Public Safety. Years later, the union continued to be a bitter pill for opponents on both sides of the issue.

Still, the department continued to professionalize and grow its ranks to a robust 160 sworn members. Savvy in their process of hiring qualified candidates who achieved high marks on the competitive civil service entrance exam, the initial list included a myriad of applicants with prior police experience. Twenty-four year-old Gary Stymiloski was one such candidate and was hired in September 1982.

Courtesy of Westchester County Department of Public Safety PBA.

A dedicated self-starter with street smarts, Gary followed his two older brothers, Paul and Edward Jr., into the world of law enforcement, serving first as a police officer in the Village of Sloatsburg, New York, for two years prior to joining the Westchester County Department.

Just months after his hiring, the youthful Gary was hand-picked to join a county-wide narcotics task force. The task force's mandate was to interdict the flow of cocaine being peddled in county high schools at an alarming rate. Gary, who graduated six years prior from Gorton High School in Yonkers, found himself back on various campuses. Gary "taught" several painful lessons to many a drug dealer about the New York State Penal Law, several of which resulted in lengthy prison sentences.

While the task force was successful and Gary's work impressive, funding was soon exhausted. Gary's efforts did not go overlooked as he was named Westchester County 'Police Officer of the Year' in 1984 by the Pulaski Association. Gary, though grateful and energized for the experience, nevertheless found himself back in the "bag" and back on patrol.

The department was responsible for policing county buildings, facilities, and parkways. One of these parkways, the Saw Mill River Parkway, was aptly named for the river it parallels. The river has the propensity to overflow following consistent rainfalls, flooding the roadway. The north-south parkway consists of four lanes separated by a rail barrier and offers limited emergency stopping space other than a wooded shoulder that lines each direction.

The serpentine-like parkway stretches 30 miles from its northern boundary in the Town of Bedford to the county's southern border with the Bronx where the Henry Hudson Parkway begins. That parkway quickly transitions into Manhattan's all-important West Side Highway.

Keeping this heavily-travelled artery open and flowing freely is a major priority for the officers who patrol it. Gary was one such officer, call sign "Sam-One." Gary's sector was from Route 117 in the Village of Elmsford to the Bronx line. Understandably, no one wants to be issued a traffic summons; yet there is a direct correlation between the number of summonses issued for excessive speed and aggressive driving on heavily travelled roadways and the significant decrease in automobile accidents that often result in serious physical injury and, many times, fatalities.

On the night of February 24, 1985, shortly past 7 p.m., Officer Stymiloski observed a vehicle operating in such a reckless manner travelling southbound on the Saw Mill River Parkway in Yonkers. The vehicle was travelling well over the posted speed limit of 50 miles per hour and first came to Gary's attention due to two lane changes where the driver failed to signal.

Gary sped up and swiftly maneuvered in behind the timeworn, two-door blue Mercury Capri, whose muffler sputtered loudly. The police car's headlights splashed over the low-to-the-ground Capri's trunk that sported a sizable decal that depicted an emblem from the wildly successful 1984 movie *Ghostbusters*.

Gary continued to shadow the vehicle and smartly waited for several minutes before activating the emergency lights on his marked Plymouth Police Interceptor.

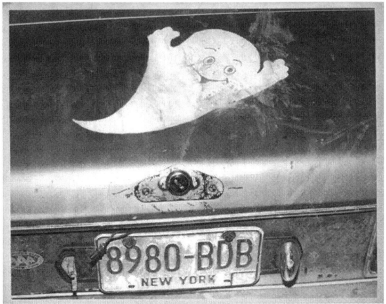

The rear of Mengel's *Ghostbuster* Capri.

The lifelong Yonkers resident knew from past experience that, just up ahead, the Palmer Road access to the parkway offered an off-ramp that afforded ample space for safely engaging in a vehicle and traffic stop.

The vehicle exited onto the access road, but failed to come to a complete stop. Gary activated the siren briefly and the car came to a halt on nearby Stratton Street. He then switched on the spotlight affixed just above his side view mirror, illuminating the interior of the stopped vehicle.

Gary observed what appeared to be three males and one female in the vehicle. The three passengers appeared jittery as they moved about in their seats, not uncommon behavior when encountering the police. The driver was unmoving, though he spied Gary through his side view mirror.

Gary promptly informed headquarters of the car stop, his location, and of the vehicle's New York State license plate, 8980BDB. He exited his patrol car and approached the Capri with a flashlight in his left hand, while his holstered four-inch .38 caliber Smith and Wesson stainless steel revolver was readily accessible at his right hip. Prior to reaching the driver's window,

4

Gary shined his flashlight into the vehicle's back seat and saw what looked like live shotgun shells on the floor.

Undaunted and fully aware that shotguns were generally legal to possess, Gary continued to the driver's door where Alex J. Mengel awaited. Mengel was 30 years old, a legal alien from Dutch Guyana who had been in the US since 1976. A tool and die maker by trade, he was the married father of a young son and lived in the Bronx.

Accompanying Mengel in the front seat was nineteen year-old Ganesh Mohan, a.k.a. Michael Mohan. Raymond Jardine and his girlfriend, Gloria Ramroop, were seated in the back. All three were immigrants from various parts of Guyana and also resided in the Bronx.

Gary surmised that someone was quite the *Ghostbusters* fan as a nearly identical decal to the one on the trunk adorned the hood of the weathered car. Gary himself had seen and enjoyed the film.

Mengel opened his door slightly to inform Gary that his window was not working. He complied when Gary requested that he exit the vehicle. Stocky and unkempt, Mengel appeared annoyed and spoke in a loud voice, questioning Gary on why he had been stopped. Not intimidated and professional as always, Gary obliged Mengel and informed him of the three traffic infractions he witnessed.

Mengel realized that this attempt at schoolyard bullying tactics had failed miserably with this officer and readily handed over the vehicle's registration. He then volunteered the fact that he and his friends were returning from camping and target shooting in the Catskills and that there were two shotguns and a rifle in the car's trunk.

The Catskills are a large area located in the southeastern part of New York about 100 miles north-northwest of New York City. The Catskills are generally defined as those areas close to or within the borders of Catskill Park, a 700,000-acre forest preserve.

Gary requested that Mengel open the truck, which he did. Gary eyeballed the weapons and Mengel offered to take the long guns out for further inspection. Gary replied that it wasn't necessary and directed him to close the trunk.

Gary asked Mengel for his driver's license and a valid insurance card. Mengel countered that he needed to search for the items within his vehicle, but assured Gary that he had a valid New York State driver's license. Mengel then stated his full name and date of birth.

Mengel leaned into the open driver's side door of his vehicle and pretended to search for the documents that Gary had requested. Nervous and agitated, he spoke, *"The cop is giving me a hard time. And he's radioing in for a license check."* Mohan, the front passenger, was fully aware that his friend never possessed a driver's license.

Now seated in his vehicle, Gary listened as the dispatcher notified him that the 1973 Mercury Capri had a valid registration in the name of Phyrween Mengel. Unknown to Gary, Phyrween was not only Alex Mengel's estranged wife, but she and her young son were in hiding from Mengel due to years of domestic abuse.

The dispatcher informed that the DMV had no driver's license on file for Alex J. Mengel. Gary, ever the optimist, queried the dispatcher again to ascertain if running the driver's name as Alexander might produce a different result. The dispatcher responded in the negative.

Officer Gary Stymiloski then made his final radio transmissions:

PO Stymiloski
"*Sam-One, Headquarters.*"

Headquarters
"*Sam-One.*"

PO Stymiloski
"*I need one unit, not an emergency, to my location.*"

Road Sergeant
"*What does he have? What does he need?*"

PO Stymiloski
"*Yeah, Sarge, no emergency. I've got a car with some shotguns in it and I want to check the car and its occupants.*"

Road Sergeant
"*Yeah, ten-four, in a few.*"

Mengel approached the police vehicle and handed Gary a Con Edison ID card from when he had been employed there as a security guard. He lied and told Gary that his wallet, along with his driver's license, had been stolen some time ago.

Gary enlightened Mengel to the fact that he was fully aware that he, Mengel, did not possess a driver's license nor a valid insurance card for the vehicle. Gary wasn't finished. He further apprised Mengel that he would be the recipient of numerous summonses and the vehicle would be impounded.

At Gary's direction, a flustered Mengel returned to his vehicle. Leaning in once more through the open door, he addressed his passengers on a whole. "*He's called for a tow truck. He's going to take us in. I'm going to shoot this guy.*"

Jardine and Ramroop responded that Mengel was crazy and that they didn't believe him.

Mengel quickly made believers of his dubious friends when he reached under his seat and brought the unregistered Star .380 black semi-automatic pistol into their view. The group was more than familiar with the weapon, all having fired it upstate just hours before. Mengel had secreted the weapon there prior to leaving for home.

He tucked the medium-framed pistol into his waistband, concealing it under his green and black winter jacket. Mengel spoke in a calm voice to Mohan, *"Michael, when you hear the shot, drive the car home."*

Mengel exited the Capri and approached Gary's police car in the same non-threatening manner he had done just minutes before. Gary, back in his vehicle was writing the first of several summonses. He saw Mengel approaching and imagined that a plea not to impound his car was forthcoming and turned his attention back to his writing.

Mengel's 1984 NYPD booking photo.

Seconds later, through the open window, the muzzle of Mengel's handgun nearly made contact with the side of Gary's head. Mengel coldly pulled the trigger once and the single .380 caliber hollow point round crashed through the left side of Gary's skull, lodging just under his right eye. The devastating wound immediately incapacitated Gary, causing irreparable damage to his central nervous system.

Hearing the shot, Mengel's disciple, Mohan, so confident that his friend would carry out the murderous act, was already positioned in the driver's seat. He followed Mengel's directive, starting the Capri and driving off. Incredulously, Raymond Jardine later told police that he never once turned around, after hearing the gun shot, but he clearly recalled that his girlfriend turned about and shrieked, " *'Oh, God.'* "

Mohan, unfamiliar with the area, drove the Capri south on Stratton Street, not realizing that the street had ended. He continued into the mouth of a nursing home parking lot. Disorientated, it took Mohan some time before he realized his mistake and finally made his way back out onto Stratton Street.

The Capri's loud muffler and suspicious activity of driving about the lot haphazardly did not go unnoticed. An alert security officer from the nursing home later reported the vehicle's actions to police, along with the gunshot that he was sure he heard just moments before observing the vehicle.

Ramroop and Jardine later recounted to police that upon reentering the roadway, they witnessed Mengel leaning into the police car through the open driver's door and that he appeared to be *"pushing the cop over so he could get in."*

Mohan entered the parkway and began driving southbound towards the Bronx. Stunningly, not one of the three witnesses to the shooting of Gary ever attempted to alert authorities to his situation as he lay dying and clearly under Mengel's control.

Even more macabre was the fact that, moments later, a police vehicle with its lights flashing passed the Bronx-bound Capri. Days later, in sworn statements to police, all three occupants concurred that Alex J. Mengel was at the wheel of that WCDPS vehicle, "Sam-One."

At approximately 7:50 p.m., the next voice heard on the WCDPS radio band was that of Gary's road sergeant, who was still responding to the location of Gary's car stop. The sergeant, who was travelling northbound on the parkway, observed a WCDPS police car, travelling southbound at high speed, its overhead lights in emergency mode.

WCDPS Radio Transcript:

Road Sergeant
"Headquarters, is Sam-One in a chase?"

Headquarters
"Negative, he requested back-up at the Palmer Road access."

Road Sergeant
"I just saw one of ours exit onto Yonkers Avenue west, looks like he's in a chase. Try to raise him."

Headquarters
"Sam-One, headquarters to Sam-One."

Within minutes, concern for Officer Gary Stymiloski's safety and whereabouts quickly turned to desperation, not only for his brother officers in the WCDPS but also for the City of Yonkers Police Department, the largest department in all of Westchester, as all attempts to communicate with or locate "Sam-One" were unsuccessful.

Complicating the search for Gary was the topography of the City of Yonkers; spread out over rising hills, its terrain rivals the City of San Francisco.

WCDPS Detective Tom McGurn, call sign "Three-Forty-Eight," was attempting to serve an arrest warrant on nearby Rumsey Road in Yonkers at the time of the incident. Unaware of the exact situation, McGurn's transmission brought a response from headquarters that conveyed the direness of the situation in trying to locate McGurn's friend, Gary.

WCDPS Radio Transcript:

Detective McGurn
"Three-Forty-Eight, Headquarters, you got something going on?"

Dispatcher
"Yeah, we've lost contact with Sam-One. We can't locate Sam-One."

In 2013, Tom McGurn retired as a patrol sergeant following a distinguished 41-year career with the WCDPS. Not only that, McGurn, a dedicated patriot, also retired from the US Army as a Chief Warrant Officer 4, who flew helicopter gunship missions in Vietnam and also during the Global War on Terrorism in Afghanistan and the War in Iraq.

McGurn recounted his feelings of disbelief upon receiving that biting transmission. *"Where was Gary? We needed to find Gary. And we needed to find him now. Everybody liked Gary. He was just a great guy and cop."*

At approximately 8:03 p.m., some thirteen minutes after the search for Gary and "Sam-One" had begun, it ended. Off-duty Yonkers Police Captain Al McEvoy, a legendary cop, who later became commissioner of the department, observed what appeared to be emergency vehicle lights reflecting off the hills in the distance. McEvoy, driving his unmarked department vehicle, had immediately joined the search for "Sam-One" after hearing the bulletin on the Yonkers Police radio band.

McEvoy continued eastbound on Yonkers Avenue towards the source of the strobe lights. He then turned south onto William Street, which was just three blocks from the Saw Mill River Parkway, as the reflection of the lights became more and more intense. The hilly street banked sharply to the left at an almost 90-degree angle and transitioned into the very narrow and even more elevated Van Buren Avenue.

Positioned on the south side of Van Buren Avenue and facing east just feet from the intersecting Prescott Street was the unaccounted for "Sam-One." Its overhead emergency lights revolved while its spotlight shone brightly into a nearby residence.

McEvoy made a brief radio notification regarding his find before exiting his vehicle. A single marked Yonkers Police car pulled in behind McEvoy's sedan. A young sergeant by the name of Larry McElroen exited the vehicle. McEvoy turned and acknowledge the patrol sergeant with a nod of his head then both men began to slowly approach "Sam-One" on either side.

Eerily, there was no one on the street. Yet the windows of the row houses were filled with curious onlookers as to why this police car, still in emergency mode, stopped in their neighborhood. The lawmen un-holstered their respective .38 caliber six-shot revolvers as they neared "Sam-One."

McEvoy scanned ahead in the hope that the unaccounted for policeman might appear and recount that his portable radio had "died" failing to transmit during a foot pursuit following the brief car chase.

It was a tunnel vision moment for McEvoy as he reached the seemingly-unoccupied police car while sirens from numerous responding police vehicles blared in the distance. The veteran cop's hopes were shattered as he peered through the open driver's side window of "Sam-One;" inside, unceremoniously positioned across the blood soaked front seat, lay the gravely wounded Gary.

McElroen, utilizing his flashlight as he approached the passenger side, had first noticed an extensive amount of blood in the back seat before he saw Gary. The scene shook both men to their very core. McElroen, though shaken, spoke calmly and clearly over his portable radio, *"Ten-thirteen, officer down. Ten-thirteen, officer down, Van Buren and Prescott."*

Seconds later, both Yonkers and WCDPS police cars packed the intersection and a dozen officers raced towards "Sam-One;" Yonkers police officers Ferrara, Cola, and Howell, aided by McElroen, pulled Gary's motionless body from the passenger seat and onto the sidewalk.

Ferrara, a member of the department's elite emergency services unit, was also cross-trained as a paramedic; he immediately began advanced life support on Gary, assisted by Howell and Cola. Another officer attempted to stem the flow of blood from Gary's devastating head wound. It was then that McElroen observed that Gary's service revolver was missing.

AA Ambulance Company containing two paramedics soon arrived on the scene to transport the unresponsive Gary to Yonkers St. Joseph's Hospital's Trauma and Emergency Care unit. The Yonkers officers continued CPR on Gary as the paramedics readied him for transport. Ferrara, along with Cola and Howell, piled into the back of the ambulance with both AA paramedics as they continued their desperate efforts to revive Gary. An unnamed Yonkers officer took the wheel of the ambulance and began a race against time to get Gary to the trauma unit.

The on-scene officers' determination in escorting the ambulance that carried their fallen comrade to the hospital in convoy fashion was palpable; the nearly fifteen police vehicles reached speeds of 80 miles per hour as they raced to block off intersections in a leap-frog tactic.

This was quite evident to McGurn when he arrived at the scene. *"When I got to Prescott and Van Buren, everybody was gone. Gary's car was there, but everybody else was gone. The overheads were off and I looked into the car - there was a pool of blood in Gary's open briefcase that was on the floor."*

McGurn secured and preserved the crime scene until other marked units relieved him.

McGurn recalled locating a nearby pay phone to call headquarters and his lieutenant answered. *"I said, hey Lou, you know they rushed Gary to the hospital. I'm still at the scene where they found him. And the lieutenant says, 'I know. Gary's gone, he's dead, Tom.'"*

WCDPS Officer George H. Farrell detailed in his official report the events that unfolded in St. Joseph's Hospital's Emergency Medicine department. Inside the trauma unit, Doctors Foder, Brittis, San Diego and Keller, aided by Officer Ferrara and numerous nurses, worked heroically for 90 minutes in their attempts to revive PO Stymiloski.

A Catholic priest administered PO Stymiloski his last rites and, at 10:08 p.m., PO Stymiloski was pronounced dead by Dr. Nardo San Diego.

The recently engaged and highly decorated Police Officer Gary Stymiloski, shield number 157, who was just entering the prime of his life, now lay dead on a cold hospital gurney.

Meanwhile, according to a local store owner's report, Mengel purchased a soft drink to refresh himself shortly after fleeing the scene.

What, exactly, was Alex J. Mengel's mindset the night he assassinated Police Officer Gary Stymiloski: that the illegal handgun he used to end Gary's life would cause him a lengthy prison sentence? Was Mengel's fear of possible deportation so great that murdering a police officer in the country that had welcomed him truly an option? Or was there something even darker at work here, something that Mengel surely needed to keep hidden from law enforcement?

How exactly did that semi-automatic pistol manufactured in the Basque Region of Spain come into Mengel's possession?

Consider Mengel's calm directive to Mohan to drive his vehicle home to the Bronx, then his cunning and devious ploy that worked to near-perfection by carjacking "Sam-One." He had thrown the proverbial wrench at police by realizing that all their resources would be utilized to search for Gary; allowing for the clean escape of both he and his friends.

Yet, he apparently lacked the intellect to figure out how to turn off the police car's emergency and spot lights that brought the full attention of the neighborhood and police to that secondary crime scene.

Then Mengel's predatory instincts surfaced once again when he decided to rob the dying young police officer of his service revolver and then disappear into the night. These actions all establish a high level of criminal sophistication that only comes from experience.

3

Every Bronx Borough Precinct of the New York City Police Department was immediately alerted to the shooting of Officer Gary Stymiloski. A city-wide BOLO was quickly issued for Mengel and the *Ghostbusters* Capri.

Word quickly reached Deputy Assistant Chief Emillio "Emil" Ciccotelli, Commander of Detectives in the Bronx. Ciccotelli, 56 years old and a 31-year veteran of the force, was an iconic figure who supervised numerous high-profile investigations and was an expert on the five organized crime families in NYC.

In 1983, the detective commander's expertise and keen insight regarding the mafia caused then US Attorney for the Southern District, Rudolph W. Giuliani, to team with Chief Ciccotelli and the detectives from his department's organized crime control bureau. Both Giuliani and Ciccotelli testified before a special hearing of the United States Senate Judiciary Committee regarding La Cosa Nostra and their troubling enterprise with Colombian narcotics traffickers.

Ciccotelli testified to the committee that the time had come for a "*major cooperative offensive*" by law enforcement against organized crime. Years later, the results of both men's call to action were apparent as the influence of the five mafia families in NYC was notably reduced, especially in the construction and garbage carting industries.

But on the night of February 24, 1985, Chief Ciccotelli, aware of Gary's shooting and that his older brother, Ed, worked as a street cop in the 48th Precinct, unleashed every resource of the NYPD in assisting the County of Westchester in the search for this 'cop shooter.'

At approximately 8:10 p.m., an anti-crime unit from the 46th Precinct located Mengel's unoccupied Capri parked opposite 2258 Grand Avenue in the Bronx, exactly where Mohan would later tell police he purposely parked the vehicle. The area was known as a hotbed for drugs and violent crime.

NYPD Officers Aguilar and Donahue spotted the Capri as they perused the area in an unmarked police car. The partners were careful not to bring attention to themselves and conducted a covert surveillance of the Capri from a safe distance. Donahue notified headquarters regarding their finding from a nearby bodega payphone.

At 10 p.m., NYPD Officers Haywood and Lane were awaiting the arrival of several WCDPS and Yonkers detectives at the Yonkers Police Detective Division. Haywood and Lane handed detectives two color photos of Mengel; one was a mugshot from his lone documented arrest by the NYPD in May 1984. The other was purportedly personally obtained by Chief Ciccotelli from members of the Mengel family.

Back in the Bronx and under the direction of Chief Ciccotelli, additional unmarked NYPD units joined in the surveillance of Mengel's car. Several marked units, along with officers from the NYPD's revered Emergency Services Unit, waited just blocks away to provide backup should anyone attempt to flee in the vehicle.

When the combined surveillance time of the vehicle reached nearly three hours, a WCDPS detective supervisor made the decision to finally end the stakeout and seize Mengel's vehicle.

Mengel's Ghostbusters Capri parked opposite
2258 Grand Avenue, Bronx.

Grand Avenue was now the site of a massive police presence, among them Detective Tom McGurn, who responded to the scene with Yonkers Detective Robert Hunt.

After a cursory inspection of the Capri from the outside to ensure that no one was secreted inside, both men, along with NYPD detectives, began to canvass the block to gain information on Mengel and anyone associated with the vehicle.

A NYPD detective lieutenant conveyed an offer of assistance from Chief Ciccotelli to a Yonkers police sergeant in that the NYPD would recover Mengel's vehicle and take it to their world-class evidence facility for processing.

The Yonkers sergeant rebuffed the NYPD official's offer in a most negative and unfiltered manner. In actuality, Mengel was now a confirmed cop killer and possibly on the loose in NYC; any offer of assistance, especially from fellow law enforcement, should have been responded to in a professional manner.

McGurn and Hunt, along with NYPD Detectives, Lambert, Morgan, and Kennedy, began to canvass the neighborhood. The detectives hit pay dirt immediately when they knocked on the door of one Subhas Singh, also a Guyanese immigrant, who lived in the basement apartment of 2258 Grand Avenue. Singh was a longtime friend of Mengel and had also participated in the weekend trip to the Catskills, but had driven home alone. Inside the apartment was Singh's wife, his three young children, and all of Mengel's travelling companions: Jardine, Ramroop and Mohan.

With the group's direct involvement unknown to the five detectives and not wanting to tip their hand, they stated Mengel had done something bad and they needed to locate him immediately.

The three said nothing about their firsthand knowledge of Mengel shooting a police officer. With the exception of Mohan, Singh, Jardine and Ramroop lied to police stating they hadn't seen Mengel in days and didn't know why his car was parked nearby.

Mohan's later statement to authorities was the most callous of all when he recounted how he silently watched an episode of *Star Trek* and simply ignored police.

Singh told detectives that Mengel and his wife previously lived in the building but had been evicted. He stated that Mengel worked sporadically for him as a car mechanic and knew him to own shotguns as he hunted with him on several occasions.

Singh volunteered Mengel's brother-in-law, Lloyd Tranquada's address and telephone number, stating Mengel had resided there some time ago. Hunt wasted no time and phoned the man. Tranquada seemed forthcoming and told Hunt that Mengel was no longer welcome at his home as he failed to pay him rent.

Tranquada also relayed names and addresses of Mengel's sister Martha, who lived in Brooklyn, and his brother Gustav, who lived in Flushing, Queens. He also added that Mengel and his wife Phyrween were to his knowledge, estranged.

Yet Singh, who at the time was apparently unaware of the gravity of Mengel's crimes, yet surely knew that something was terribly amiss.

Especially when Jardine, Ramroop, and Mohan arrived at his apartment, appeared shaken and said little. Regardless, Singh knowingly withheld vital information regarding his and the trio's involvement with Mengel over the weekend.

The detectives immediately sensed that these people were involved on some level and were at the very least protecting Mengel. Unaware of the exact diabolical chain of events, the detectives from Westchester surmised that Mengel, fled the scene of the initial car stop with Gary in close pursuit. Mengel then somehow and possibly with assistance managed to outmaneuver Gary, shooting him on Van Buren Avenue and escaped to the Bronx.

The detectives' next move would be to request, or if necessary, insist that the group, minus Singh's wife and children, accompany them to the 46th Precinct in the Bronx to gain further information on Mengel. Once out of their comfort zone and separated in individual interview rooms in a police precinct, Mengel's friends would find out just how serious the murder of a police officer was perceived in the US.

This was not to be as WCDPS Detective Lieutenant Richard Crawford, who followed detectives inside, announced that the group had given police enough information for now. He then ordered the detectives back out to Mengel's vehicle, which he viewed as the investigation's top priority.

Tom McGurn remembers the looks of disbelief from his contemporaries and being dumbfounded by the decision. *These people obviously knew more than they were giving up and we had a dead cop. They should have been charged with at least hindering a prosecution and possibly even conspiracy.*

Meanwhile, back in Yonkers at both the location of the car stop of Mengel and where "Sam-One" was eventually located, a sea of uniformed officers and detectives scoured the areas for any trace of Mengel, evidence, and witnesses.

Underlining the gravity of the situation, a civil defense unit was requested by authorities; the unit responded with massive generator-powered spotlights that illuminated both crime scenes.

In actuality, the murder of Officer Gary Stymiloski involved three crime scenes: Stratton Street, the intersection of Van Buren Avenue and Prescott Street, and the police vehicle, "Sam-One," itself a virtual moving crime scene. There is no record of such an incident involving a uniformed on-duty police officer in United States history.

County cop killed in Yonkers shooting

Police officials examine the patrol car of slain officer Gary Stymiloski. The car, with the fatally wounded officer in it, was found on the corner of Van Buren and Prescott streets in Yonkers.

Less than an hour after Gary's death, Westchester County Assistant District Attorney Bruce Bendish, who was also the chief prosecutor of the homicide unit, arrived at the "Sam-One" crime scene along with 'Brass' from both departments. Bendish and WCDPS Commissioner Anthony Mosca sadly viewed the blood-drenched interior of the fallen officer's police car; along with Yonkers Police Detectives, Captain Owen McClain and Lieutenant Jack Roach.

McClain was a politically-savvy 36-year veteran who had fought as a US Marine in World War II. He also experienced two line-of-duty murders of fellow Yonkers police officers during his time on the force.

Roach was also a former Marine with over twenty years on the force and was a rare breed of cop; highly thought of by his superiors and respected by the rank and file. More importantly he was a top-notch detective and supervisor. McClain immediately tasked Roach, who supervised all major case investigations in the city with hunting down Gary's killer, regardless of jurisdictional issues.

Before midnight, it was mutually agreed upon by Bendish and both departments that Roach would directly supervise a joint task force of detectives from both agencies to investigate Gary's murder. He would report daily to both McClain and WCDPS Deputy Commissioner Tom Sweeney.

Roach quickly tapped one of his best detectives, Vinny Patalano, a veteran homicide investigator, to partner with WCDPS's lead detective, 34 year-old Mike DeRosa. The two investigators would not sleep for nearly 30 hours.

DeRosa, now retired some thirteen years is an interesting study; a dedicated cop, who later as a detective sergeant supervised the largest drug bust in Westchester County history at the time, is gracious and self-deprecating as he sits in his upstate New York home. Yet the feeling is perceptible on this early October afternoon, that he would much rather be riding the Harley Davidson Road King, that sits in the garage of his Florida home.

"There had been several street robberies in and around the White Plains Train Station for some weeks. So on the evening of Gary's shooting, I set up in the parking lot looking for bad guys when I heard the radio traffic about Sam-One.

Straight away, I knew that something was very, very wrong. I started down the Bronx River Parkway in my unmarked Plymouth Fury that, by the way, had no dashboard light or siren. I just put on my four-way flashers and blew my horn the whole way down to Yonkers."

A Yonkers uniformed officer's thorough canvass of Prescott Street provided Patalano and DeRosa with their first up-close witness of Mengel after he fled from "Sam-One."

The married daughter of a family-owned neighborhood deli recounted how a man, who fit Mengel's description, entered the store just around 8 p.m. The man seemed nervous as police cars with their red lights flashing sped past the store. He spoke with a strange foreign accent and was drenched in perspiration, which she thought was odd for a winter's night. He also clutched an old rag or towel that was wrapped around something. Mengel paid for a soft drink, gulped it down, left the store, and proceeded in the direction away from where the police cars were headed.

Back on Grand Avenue in the Bronx, Detective Hunt's next move was to enter Mengel's locked Capri. The detective's reason in doing so was solely for practical purposes, not evidentiary. With the assistance of an NYPD Emergency Services officer, the driver's door was slim-jimmied opened. Hunt leaned ever so carefully into the vehicle and immediately took notice of several live shotgun rounds, along with a pair of handcuffs that rested on the front passenger floor mat and an empty brown handgun holster that was stuffed into the driver's door pocket.

Hunt then placed the standard engine's stick shift in neutral and released the parking brake to allow for free movement of the soon-to-be impounded vehicle.

The vehicle was then impounded by Yonkers Police to their third floor garage at police headquarters.

In the early morning hours of Monday, February 25th, Roach, Patalano, and DeRosa responded to the residence of Yonkers Criminal Court Judge, the Honorable Emmett J. Murphy, where they secured a signed search warrant for Mengel's Capri.

Shortly after, the three task force detectives were standing by Mengel's vehicle as two Yonkers detectives, both specialists in evidence recovery, entered. Besides the articles that Detective Hunt had observed in plain sight earlier, more troubling items were recovered from inside the vehicle that stunned investigators.

One item, a road map, literally portended to lead detectives to unsolved or yet-to-be uncovered crimes committed by Mengel. But their first priority was to capture him as quickly as possible.

4

Just hours after the sun came up on February 25th, Patalano and DeRosa were positive that Gary was shot on Stratton Street and that Mengel carjacked "Sam-One," while Gary lay dying inside. Moreover, the detectives realized that Mengel was assisted.

No one interviewed during the canvass on Van Buren Avenue or Prescott Street reported hearing a gunshot. Yet back on Stratton Street, a married couple informed DeRosa, that they arrived back at their home last evening, at approximately 7:45. Less than a hundred feet from their front step, they saw a county police officer in the midst of a traffic stop of a small dark vehicle.

The couple went on to recount that a man, presumably the driver, who fit Mengel's description was at the rear of the vehicle talking to the officer. They couldn't confirm if there were passengers in the car. Minutes after entering their home, they heard what sounded like a "*loud bang.*" The wife informed DeRosa how moments later, she looked out of her front window and watched the county police car speed off onto the parkway. The dark car was already gone.

The couple's story and timeline matched the security guard's account from the nursing home to near perfection; it also validated the detectives' belief that Mengel carjacked "Sam-One" and that a passenger in Mengel's vehicle had driven the Capri from the scene and back to the Bronx.

Bolstering the detectives' theory was a Van Buren Avenue resident, who informed police that she had at first mistaken the county police car for a taxi but then clearly recognized it for what it was. She added that a man, not in a uniform, stepped out backwards from the driver's door, closed it and then ran towards Prescott Street.

At 9 a.m. Patalano and DeRosa briefed Roach in regards to their findings at the Yonkers Detective Division. Though Roach still fumed after learning of the WCDPS supervisor's investigatory blunder inside the Bronx apartment; he knew his detectives' conclusions were absolutely correct.

At some point during the gut-wrenching night, Roach received a cassette tape of the WCDPS radio transmissions. Gary clearly stated "*occupants*" in regards to his car stop along with something else that captured Roach's attention, "*shotguns.*" Still, they had no witness that could ID or for that fact confirm that anyone else was present in Mengel's vehicle.

"*We can now, boss,*" came the voice of Yonkers Detective James Kirkwood as he entered through Roach's open office door. Kirkwood, 37, a recent addition to Roach's 'A-Team' of investigators, had also worked through the night.

He was following up on an early morning tip to the detective division in regards to Gary's shooting and had just returned from interviewing the caller. She told Kirkwood that while stopped at the intersection of Stratton Street and Yorkshire Place; she witnessed a small dark vehicle stopped in front of a county police car with its lights flashing. She also recalled observing persons in the front and rear passenger seats, possibly males.

She ended her account by telling Kirkwood that as she drove through the intersection she saw a man fitting Mengel's general description interacting with the police officer at the rear of the dark car.

Roach was now certain that at least two of the people reported to be in that Bronx apartment last evening were involved in Gary's murder. He directed the three detectives in his office along with a half a dozen more to locate and re-interview all those individuals, forthwith.

5

On the morning of February 25, 44 year-old Beverly Capone, the divorced mother of an adult daughter, left her comfortable Westchester home in Mount Vernon for her position as an IBM computer programmer supervisor.

Attractive and petite at just 5'1, Beverly entered her newly-purchased white 1985 Toyota Tercel four-door sedan. Beverly's half-hour commute to work was a bit more enjoyable now in her new vehicle. The office was located just off the Saw Mill River Parkway in the serene Village of Dobbs Ferry, some seven miles north of Yonkers.

Conversely, Alex Mengel spent most of this morning and the night before attempting to stay warm while holed up in a dilapidated storage shed on the property of the Yonkers Motor Inn. The motel had been smartly erected just yards from where the two parkways that Beverly Capone regularly travelled on intersected. The motel's main entrance lied on the very busy thoroughfare of Yonkers Avenue.

It seemed fitting that the hunted cop killer sought shelter at this motor inn that had long ago been overrun by junkies, pimps, and their prostitutes, along with every other reprobate imaginable. The motel was once a welcomed overnight respite for vacationers and business travelers on their way to or from NYC, but the city's illicit drug enterprise had eventually spilled over into Yonkers.

Though police searched the motor inn and its grounds before he took refuge there, Mengel was less than a half mile away from where he had abandoned "Sam-One" and a mortally-wounded Gary.

Mengel, who was purportedly an experienced outdoorsman and hunter, moved just after first light. He travelled on foot a short distance along an abandoned railroad line that was concealed by woods just off Yonkers Avenue. He then traced northward along the frigid west side of the Saw Mill River.

6

Flushing, Queens, New York

Flushing is best known for being the home of Major League Baseball's New York Mets and the annual host of the US Open Tennis Tournament. Yet the famous neighborhood was once a forerunner to Hollywood, Headquarters of the United Nations from 1946 to 1949, was the site of two World Fairs and of course, the home of the 1969 Super Bowl Champion New York Jets.

On July 16, 1984, along with its rich history, Flushing was also a good place for hard-working couples to live and raise a family. Twelve year-old Antonella Mattina came from such a family. Antonella, the happy-go-lucky daughter of a painting contractor, was looking forward to entering the seventh grade in September. Antonella's mother, Maria, finally acquiesced to her daughter's numerous pleas on that summer morning to be entrusted with her first 'big girl' errand and to do so alone.

Bright and responsible beyond her years, Antonella successfully deposited checks on behalf of the family business at the local Citibank. The branch located in the Linden Vue Shopping Center at the intersection of Willet and Parson Boulevards' was just blocks from her home. The five-foot tall, 90-pound, and brown-eyed Antonella was never seen alive again.

Antonella's disappearance triggered one of the most massive searches in NYC history. Hundreds of officers from numerous NYPD commands to include K-9 units, harbor patrol, and aviation units, virtually scoured the entire city for Antonella to no avail.

Within a month, the reward for information on Antonella reached $20,000. Prayer vigils for her safe return were held weekly at her local parish, the Church of St. Mel. Hundreds of volunteers posted more than 10,000 color flyers (the first of their kind) of the missing girl's picture and information throughout NYC and surrounding municipalities.

NYPD Detective Walter "Bill" Clarke of the 109th Precinct was the lead investigator on the case. It was a bitter and frustrating case for the celebrated detective who, years later, gained fame in Hollywood, first as a technical advisor then as an executive producer on the long-running and very popular TV series *NYPD Blue*.

Weeks later, with no sign of Antonella, John Mallon, whose company, IBI Security Service Inc., pledged $10,000 toward the reward remarked, "*A civilized society should not accept that children simply disappear. We want to keep the case alive and before the public, and I think money talks*"

On Monday morning, February 25, 1985, the late edition of every New York metro area newspaper reported on Gary's murder and plastered Mengel's mugshot along with the *Ghostbusters* Capri across their front pages.

Among the hundreds of calls that police in Westchester received, one was from Phyrween Mengel, who saw her name in the *New York Post*, listed as the registered owner of the Capri. Phyrween, who was living discreetly in Richmond, Queens, under the auspices of a NYC domestic violence program (the first of its kind in the country) wanted to clear herself of any involvement in Gary's murder at once.

A different and most unexpected call was placed to the NYPD's 109th Precinct. A local resident stated that the newspaper picture of Mengel, looked very much like the man, that he reported to police seeing with Antonella Mattina, on the day she disappeared.

7

At 11 a.m. while other task force detectives sought out the 'Bronx Four' Kirkwood along with WCDPS Detective Jack Clarke arrived at the Flushing home of Alex Mengel's older brother, Gustav Mengel. The three-family residence had been under police surveillance since shortly before midnight as were all of Mengel's relative's homes in the metropolitan area.

Gustav stated that he had not seen Alex since before last Christmas. He further said he had no idea of his brother's whereabouts. He then volunteered that his brother had several garbage bags of personal belongings in the garage of his home and freely turned them over.

The detectives then skillfully queried Mengel with regard to the name Christine Murphy. The question was in reference to a New York State driver's license with that same name and a Flushing address that was found inside "Sam-One."

Gustav paused. He then answered that he did know someone by that name and that she used to live in a building he owns in Flushing. He continued that she moved out three years ago and he hadn't seen her since.

The detectives already knew the answer as NYPD detectives had responded to the address on the license just hours after Gary's murder to check on Ms. Murphy's welfare. The account from the superintendent of that residence was nearly exact to Mengel's.

Subhas Singh was clearly rattled when Detectives DeRosa and Hunt appeared at his front door just before noon. Singh, struggled to comport himself as he continued to lie about not being in Mengel's company over the past weekend.

He was more than relieved when the detectives turned their questions to where Raymond Jardine lived and worked. Singh told them Jardine lived just upstairs and was at his job as a salesman at a Manhattan shoe store.

The detectives' further canvassed the neighborhood, showing pictures of Mengel and the *Ghostbusters* Capri to residents and Passersby; many of whom recognized Mengel and his car from the area but had no further information.

DeRosa and Hunt after following up on several other leads, returned to the Bronx later in the evening to speak with Raymond Jardine. He never arrived.

The task force's level of commitment was clear as they followed up on every lead. Detectives went to the county offices of Con Edison to investigate the ID card that Mengel handed to Gary during the car stop and was recovered inside "Sam-One." A company official confirmed that Mengel had worked there briefly some time ago as a security guard. They also furnished investigators with a recently retired employee's name and address, whom Mengel had listed as a personal reference on his application.

When questioned by detectives, the retiree, who also lived in the Bronx, categorically denied knowing Alex Mengel or anyone else by that last name and was truly mystified that Mengel used her as a reference.

8

On the afternoon of February 25th, Phyrween Mengel met with Roach and Patalano at Yonkers Police Headquarters. Phyrween provided investigators with some pedigree and preliminary information. She then said she had been estranged from Mengel since last April 30th, following the worst beating that she had ever suffered at his hands.

The fractured jaw that sent a fearful Phyrween to a Bronx hospital emergency room that evening, combined with her fragmented account of an alleged street mugging, raised classic red flags of domestic violence, causing hospital staff to contact police. Mengel was located and arrested by the NYPD on May 2nd.

She went on to tell task force detectives that though the car was registered in her name, it was Alex's car and that he exercised total control over it. Phyrween confided that this was the first time since she had been married that she had known peace and simply wanted to raise her young son in the same manner and without Mengel.

Detectives knew Phyrween was a treasure trove of knowledge regarding Mengel's psyche and habits; a knowledge that they hoped would expedite their search and capture of him.

Phyrween informed them that most of her husband's friends were in the Kingsbridge section of the Bronx. She added that she only knew the first names of his friends; the list included Sabhas (Singh), Michael (Mohan), Raymond (Jardine), Raymond's girlfriend Gloria (Ramroop), and an Andrew from New Jersey.

Phyrween, though victimized by Mengel for years, was still the mother of his child. She was silently overwhelmed by his level of violence and the crimes that he was now suspected of. She tired quickly but readily assured police that she would aid them in their search for Mengel and gather as much information as possible on his friends and associates, including last names, addresses and telephone numbers.

Phyrween's mention of an Andrew from New Jersey would prove prophetic.

9

On the morning of February 26th. Subhas Singh answered the knock on his apartment door to find a familiar face, Detective Hunt who wasn't alone. Accompanying him was WCDPS Detective Sergeant Mike Flaherty. They both had more questions for him.

Singh stepped out into the hallway and closed his door, barely muffling the sounds of a crying baby. Hunt asked him to recount his story again about his activities of the last weekend. Though Singh believed these policemen saw right through his lies, he held his fear in check and retold his untruths. The pressure must have been unbearable for Singh as he wondered if a visit from the police was going to be a daily occurrence.

The detectives knew he was holding back and it was only a matter of time. Once again the conversation switched to the whereabouts of Raymond Jardine. Singh was glad to finally utter a truthful sentence and stated that he hadn't seen Jardine since Sunday night.

Before leaving the Bronx to seek out Jardine at his workplace in Manhattan, Hunt and Flaherty paid a visit to Michael Mohan's family home. To Hunt's surprise, Mohan identified himself by his formal name, Ganesh Mohan, although everyone else that Hunt had spoken to referred to the nineteen year old as Michael or Mike.

Hunt's memory regarding Mohan's demeanor on Sunday night was crystal clear. He recalled the contemptuous look on the teen's face the two or three times he looked up at police and away from the TV.

Recess was over, Hunt thought as he informed Mohan of his Miranda Rights and that the rest of his questioning would take place at the 46th. Precinct.

Hunt's ruse worked to perfection as the confident look on Mohan's face vanished. A short time later, Mohan and the two detectives from Westchester crossed swords inside an interview room courtesy of the 46th Detective Squad.

Mohan's flawed tale had more holes in it than the front nine and for that matter the back nine as well. Even when confronted by the clear inconsistencies between his story, Singh's account and Jardine's version that was documented on Sunday night; Mohan refused to come clean.

With Mohan's permission, Hunt snapped a Polaroid photo of him. Then they drove him home, once there the detectives asked to inspect the three shotguns owned by Mohan, Hunt then copied down the weapon's serial numbers.

An hour later Hunt and Flaherty were standing in the mid-town shoe store that Singh referenced, looking for Jardine. The manager informed them that Jardine had requested to move to one of the chain's satellite stores and was now working in the north Bronx location.

Another hour passed before they were finally face to face with a surprised Jardine. Jardine repeated his cover story from Sunday night; stating the last time he saw Mengel was on Friday night.

Jardine continued that on Sunday evening at 7 p.m. he and Gloria went down stairs to Singh's apartment to watch a cowboy movie. When queried by Flaherty if he knew his friend, Mengel to own a handgun, Jardine lied again and said he believed Mengel owned a pellet gun.

Hunt, asked Jardine if he had more than one address. Jardine replied, no, and that he lived just above his friend Singh's apartment at 2258 Grand Avenue with his fiancée, Gloria Ramroop.

Following the interview Hunt called Roach to inform him that they had finally located Jardine and that his alibi was nearly as weak as Mohan's.

10

Andrew Remdas (the Andrew that Phyrween Mengel referenced) walked into WCDPS headquarters at 5 p.m. on Tuesday, February 26. Remdas was not alone; he was accompanied by his girlfriend, Audrey Bastian, and they both had a story to tell regarding an acquaintance by the name of Alex Mengel.

Twenty minutes later, the New Jersey couple was escorted to Yonkers police headquarters and recounted their story to Roach and DeRosa.

Remdas told the detectives how he and Audrey had met his friends Raymond Jardine and Gloria Ramroop at a tavern in Rutherford, New Jersey, the previous Friday night, February 22. Alex Mengel, who they had met just once before, was also there along with a Michael Mohan and a girl, who went by the name of Grace.

The group discussed the camping trip they were about to embark on that weekend. Audrey had a prior engagement on Saturday evening in the Bronx so it was agreed upon that they would pick up Jardine and Ramroop after the affair and head up to the Town of Cairo, located in the Catskills, later that night.

In separate sworn statements, Remdas and Bastian told police how they, along with Jardine and Ramroop, arrived after 2 a.m. on Sunday morning in the area of Cairo. Unsure of exactly where their friends' campsite was, they decided to sleep in their car. At some time around 7:30 a.m., the two couples awoke to the sound of a car with a loud muffler. The car, a blue two-door Mercury Capri, sported two large *Ghostbuster* emblems and was driven by Alex Mengel.

Due to the rough terrain and the fact that the Capri was already mud-covered and in some disrepair, Mengel ferried the group to the campsite where Michael Mohan and Sabhas Singh awaited. The couple shared how the group spent much of the day following breakfast, hiking, small game hunting and then target shooting at bottles and cans; first with a .22 caliber rifle, then with a handgun that Mengel drew from his waistband.

Remdas believed the weapon to be a 9mm semiautomatic pistol that featured a dark finish and brown wooden handles. He fired the handgun three or four times while Bastian fired only one round, but she distinctly recalled that the weapon was ultimately returned to Mengel.

Remdas bolstered his girlfriend's recollection by stating that he remembered seeing Mengel secret the handgun back into his waistband.

The couple continued their eye-opening story, informing that the entire group left the area at about 6 p.m. on Sunday evening. Singh drove alone in his vehicle while Mohan, Jardine, and Ramroop accompanied Mengel in the *Ghostbusters* Capri.

Bastian, unsure of the exact route back home, began to follow the cars driven by Mengel and Singh. As the small convoy approached the Rip Van Winkle Bridge, Remdas remembered telling Bastian to slow down as both Mengel and Singh were driving much too fast to follow.

To the detectives' amazement, Bastian then correctly recited the license plate of Mengel's Capri, having considered it a good number to play.

Although Roach was overjoyed with the young couple's willingness to come forward and their candidness in supplying such a monumental break in the case, he was equally incensed by what he had just heard. He thanked the young couple for their help and politely excused himself from the interview room. The veteran detective supervisor found it hard to believe that three people had witnessed a police officer's murder and said absolutely nothing.

Roach paged Detective Hunt. Upon Hunt's call back, Roach told him to turn around and pick up Jardine. He then directed several detectives from the task force to pick up Singh, Mohan and Ramroop. He further instructed that anyone who chose to not come willingly was to be placed in handcuffs immediately and transported to his office.

Back in the interview room, Remdas told DeRosa how Bastian was the catalyst for coming forward to police, having purchased a late edition of the *New York Daily News* on Monday morning in New Jersey and reading about Gary's murder. Bastian was shocked when she saw the picture of the *Ghostbusters* car that looked exactly like the vehicle apparently owned by their acquaintance known as Alex.

Unsure of Mengel's last name, she immediately called Remdas and asked if he had seen the story on the murdered cop in Yonkers. Remdas stated he had not but told Bastian Alex's last name was, in fact, Mengel. Bastian then informed Remdas that Alex had apparently murdered a police officer.

Remdas set off quickly to purchase a newspaper of his own.

Armed with details from the paper, Remdas began making phone calls; his first that evening was to Michael Mohan. Mohan stated that he knew about the police officer being shot. When Remdas pressed him for further details as for reasons why, Mohan ended the call. Remdas then phoned Singh, who said he read about it in the papers but knew nothing else.

The next morning, the couple called a friend of Bastian's who was in law enforcement in New Jersey. This unnamed official escorted the couple to WCDPS headquarters.

Unknown to task force detectives was at the same time they were interviewing the couple from New Jersey, Beverly Capone's daughter, 22 year-old Pamela Capone, was in the process of filing a missing person's report of her mother with the Mount Vernon Police Department. Capone and her white Toyota Tercel had not been seen since leaving her office on Monday evening.

11

By 8 p.m. all four of Mengel's friends were sitting in separate interview rooms within WCDPS headquarters. Mohan, Jardine, and Singh had been immediately picked up in the Bronx; while Ramroop, who was employed in New Jersey was intercepted by detectives as she approached her doorstep.

The situation was quite different now. All four subjects were informed that they could be prosecuted for an assortment of serious crimes or be classified as material witnesses and placed in protective custody at the Westchester County Jail for an undetermined amount of time - or they could simply cooperate with detectives.

Singh, out of apparent shame and fear for his family's future, was the first to come clean. He told police about that weekend trip to the campsite in the Catskills and how he and Mengel hunted in the Cairo and East Durham areas numerous times over the years. He then recounted fervently how he drove home alone Sunday night from upstate and that he was nowhere near Mengel or the other three at the time of Gary's murder.

Conversely, Mohan and Ramroop only cooperated after lengthy jail sentences were assured, along with the promise of deportation back to their country of origin after the completion of their sentences. Still, after all this, Ramroop was still hiding something.

Jardine, who also had a secret of his own, continued with his flawed attempt at deception by stating that he was not even in Mengel's car at the time of the murder. He then went too far and foolishly voiced his annoyance at being harassed by police. Detective DeRosa, who was alone with Jardine in that second floor interview room, was not in the mood for such games.

"These people had already impeded our investigation for forty-eight hours and Mengel was still on the loose. The Stymiloski family was planning a funeral for one of our brother officers and he still wanted to be cute," DeRosa recalled thinking.

"The days following Gary's murder were very warm after a bitterly cold winter so all the windows in the office were open. I had enough of his crap so I grabbed him [Jardine] by the scruff of his neck and rag-dolled him over to the open window.

"Okay, you're going to tell me everything you know or you're going out this window. I had him about halfway out when he says, 'Okay, I'll tell you what really happened.'"

Following the "bonding" session between he and DeRosa, Jardine detailed in a sworn statement how Mengel murdered Gary and of his own involvement in the incident along with the lies that followed.

The four were then taken to the Yonkers Police Impound Garage where Mengel's Capri was stored. Mohan, Jardine and Ramroop made additional sworn statements identifying that blue1973 Mercury Capri as the vehicle that Mengel had driven them in on that fateful night. Singh also identified that vehicle as the same car that his friend, Alex Mengel drove from the East Durham campsite on February 24th.

Roach alerted task force commanders of the groundbreaking information. On the morning of February 27th a section of the task force under the joint command of Detective Captain McClain and Deputy Commissioner Sweeney arrived in Cairo. The detectives were met by investigators from the New York State Police Bureau of Criminal Investigation (BCI).

DeRosa had made such a lasting impression on Jardine that he volunteered to personally accompany police to the Cairo area and point out locations and areas that he knew Mengel frequented.

Shortly after 8 a.m. that morning, Yonkers Police Detective Vinny Lenci recovered three .380 caliber shell casings next to a stone wall in a wooded area across from the Lamp Post Motel in Cairo. The ballistic fingerprint on the shell casings recovered were later positively identified as coming from Mengel's Star .380 semi-automatic handgun, the weapon used to kill Gary.

Though the detective's find was vital to the case, still there was no sign of Mengel in any of the areas that the contingent of lawmen searched for him.

Hours later and some 160 miles west of Cairo in the Village of Skaneateles, New York, a thirteen year-old newspaper delivery girl was walking her route on East Street. A small white car pulled alongside her. The driver, a woman with longish dark hair, asked for directions as she peered down at a road map perched on her lap.

Eager to help, the young girl started towards the car. Just feet away, she stopped cold. Although the driver wore a dress, lipstick and an apparent wig, the girl immediately recognized this person to be a man disguised as a woman. As the young girl began to slowly back away, the driver produced a handgun and pointed it at the terrified girl. *"Get in the car or I'll kill you,"* the man calmly stated. Instead the girl turned and dashed off, fleeing up the nearby driveway of one of her customer's homes as the man in the white car drove off.

The girl described the man to police as white and who spoke with a strange foreign accent.

State police investigators responded to the young girl's home later that evening. With the permission of her parents, investigators asked the girl to view a photo array. The array was composed of six photos that included

Mengel and five other men of a similar likeness. Though Mengel had been in disguise when she encountered him, the teen immediately picked out his photo, positively identifying Mengel, as the man in the white car.

12

Mengel walked all day to reach a fishing spot off the Saw Mill River Parkway that he recalled visiting with Mohan and Singh. A popular restaurant, La Cantina, was also situated in that area; its parking lot ended just feet from the water and overlooked V.E. Macy Park.

Mengel was concealed by snow-covered tree branches between the parking lot's edge and water. Mengel, tired and hungry after having battled the elements for over 24 hours and not equipped for ice fishing, turned human predator once more as he focused his sights on the restaurant's parking lot. He watched as a seemingly-unending flow of cars containing well-attired restaurant patrons arrived just after dark filling the parking lot

Although there were substantial targets of opportunity, Mengel knew that too much activity was a dangerous thing that could compromise him.

Conversely, the parking lot of the IBM Satellite office, located on Lawrence Street in Dobbs Ferry, approximately a mile and a half away from La Cantina, contained few cars, was poorly lit and had little activity.

Beverly Capone worked late on Monday night, February 25, not leaving until 8 p.m. A co-worker asked Beverly if she had any plans for the evening. Beverly simply answered, *"I'm taking these old bones home."*

Mengel's first thought was of hot-wiring the brand new white Toyota and making his escape. But then Mengel, the cunning, hunted man, surmised a hostage, preferably a woman, could provide great cover for himself while on the run.

Minutes later, Mengel watched from the shadows as a lone silhouetted figure exited the building and started towards the white Toyota. As Beverly came into full view just feet from her car, Mengel was overjoyed; he couldn't have hoped for a more perfect target than the petite and business attired woman.

As Beverly unlocked her car door, Mengel surprised her from behind at gunpoint. Terrified, Beverly obeyed Mengel's orders as he hustled her over and into the front passenger seat, closing the door. Mengel wasn't worried about Beverly fleeing from the vehicle as he made his way around the car and into the driver's seat. In fact, he had entered the vehicle earlier and jerry-rigged the front passenger door to not open from the inside.

DeRosa recounted that when Yonkers evidence detectives completed their thorough processing and work-up of Mengel's Capri, besides the disturbing items that were invoiced, there was one mechanical peculiarity: the front passenger's door had been purposely disabled not to open from the inside.

"This was obviously a major part of his M.O.," DeRosa stated.

What went through Mengel's mind during the two-hour drive north as he listened to radio news reports that he was now the most wanted man in New York, having been placed on that list by Governor Mario M. Cuomo hours before?

More terrifying, what was going through the mind of Beverly Capone, now the hostage of a cop killer?

13

On the morning of Thursday, February 28, the task force briefly turned their attention away from their investigation into the murder of Police Officer Gary Stymiloski to attend his 'Full Inspector's funeral.'

Shortly before noon, an escort of some 60 police motorcycles led the Stymiloski funeral motorcade up North Broadway in Hastings-on-Hudson. As the motorcade came to a stop, the Westchester County Police Emerald Society Pipe Band's muffled drums began to solemnly beat.

A sea of over 5,000 law enforcement officers from twenty states and Canada snapped to attention and saluted as the flag-draped casket containing the body of the 27 year-old murdered police officer was carried before them and into North Yonkers Community Church.

Gary's parents, Dorothea and Edward Sr., were helped into the church by their daughter, Lori, and their police officer sons, Paul and Edward Jr. Following closely behind was Gary's fiancée, Karen Parks, and other Stymiloski family members.

275 officers from the WCDPS, 90 percent of the force, along with numerous county and various other public officials filled in the rest of the 400-seat church.

"We know the reality and violence of how he died," the Reverend L. Lester McGonagle said during the service. *"Any one of the police officers inside or outside of this church could have been Gary. That's why they are here, to show their oneness at the precariousness of their vocation.*

Gary's coffin rested dramatically in front of a wide window behind the altar, set against the backdrop of the Palisades across the Hudson River.

The reverend recounted Gary's life, his upbringing in Yonkers and plans for a November wedding. *"His life has been shortened, negated by a violent act committed by someone who, in a single moment, changed a destiny."*

As Gary's coffin was carried from the church, his brothers walked behind the coffin, one of them carrying his cap, badge and gloves. Gary was buried in Mount Hope Cemetery in Hastings on Hudson.

Meanwhile, one case on the other side of the county was rapidly gaining notoriety: the missing person's case of Beverly Capone. A plethora of TV News outlets and newspapers were now covering the story of the unexplained disappearance of the IBM supervisor and mother that police had no leads on.

14

On the morning of Friday, March 1, Mohan and Singh accompanied Detectives Kirkwood and Clarke to the Cairo/East Durham area in an attempt to identify additional places that Mengel frequented and could be possibly hiding in.

By 9:30 a.m. State Police BCI Investigators Fred Grunwald and Bill Fitzmaurice were escorting the group.

Being familiar with the area, Singh was encouraged to direct the group's movement. Singh took officials to several wooded areas adjacent to the main road, Route 145, where he and Mengel hunted. The search included several cabins and motels but showed no signs of Mengel.

Singh recalled another house on a ridge overlooking a creek opposite a heavily wooded area where he and Mengel hunted deer. Fitzmaurice replied that he believed he knew the location of that house. He then disclosed that he had checked the premises there on Wednesday and found a glass pane in the rear door broken out, and an inner door unlocked, but no one inside.

Kirkwood and Clarke traded glances of disbelief, causing Fitzmaurice to qualify his statement. The veteran investigator explained that it was not uncommon for local teenagers to break into houses and cabins over the winter, as nearly all vacation properties closed up after hunting season and didn't reopen until late spring.

Nevertheless, the detectives wanted to see the house and surrounding area that had been important enough for Singh to remember.

Fitzmaurice drove them down a rutted and slippery back country road. Singh assured investigators that this was the place he remembered.

When detectives entered the house, it was in disarray; a pot containing the remnants of soup was found on the kitchen table along with several empty food cans. Fitzmaurice informed that this was the condition he had found the residence in just two days prior.

Fitzmaurice led the detectives into the living room where there was a damaged jukebox with its coin box removed. Kirkwood and Clarke did a cursory inspection of the rest of the cabin that contained one bedroom and a bath. Still, there was no definitive sign of Mengel.

Upon arriving back at the trooper barracks, Kirkwood called Roach to update him on their search. He told Roach about the burglarized home that Singh had directed them to. Roach didn't believe in coincidences and directed Kirkwood to request that state investigators have their crime scene unit process that residence as soon as possible.

15

Transcript of Buffalo Police Homicide Unit telephone conversation on March 1 at 11:15 p.m.:

"Buffalo Homicide, Detective Sergeant Gorski."

"I have information about the person responsible for killing a cop in New York City," the apparent male teenager with a nervous Bronx accent stated.

"He left for Toronto," the caller continued while a female voice of a similar age was heard speaking in the background apparently coaching the male caller.

The female then took control of the call and stated, *"I think the killing happened in the Bronx."*

"Can you give me his name or description?" Detective Sergeant Gorski queried.

"I don't know his name, but my friend does. He came to Buffalo after the killing."

Gorski reported that the caller then hung up. Minutes later, Gorski, after speaking with both the New York City Police and state police called the Yonkers Police Detective Division.

As Detective Patalano entered his office the next morning, he was immediately apprised of the call from Buffalo Homicide by the night watch detective.

Patalano wasted no time and reached out to DeRosa. Believing the call to have some validity, both detectives began a telephone canvass of their witness list to ascertain if Mengel had any connection to the Buffalo area.

Andrew Remdas once again proved valuable. Remdas informed Patalano that Mengel, through his married sister, did know a Troy Tranquada, and Remdas believed he was a current student at the University of Buffalo. Patalano then recalled seeing that last name on an early task force report. In fact, Yonkers Detective Hunt had spoken to Tranquada's father, Lloyd, the night of Gary's murder.

Realizing how many of Mengel's associates had already obstructed the investigation, Patalano opted not to call the Tranquada family but instead to reach out directly to Buffalo Homicide.

Within two hours, University of Buffalo junior Troy Tranquada was sitting in a homicide interview room at Buffalo Police Headquarters.

Tranquada confirmed to police that he had met with Alex Mengel inside a car that Mengel operated in one of the university parking lots on Thursday afternoon, February 28.

Tranquada went on to tell investigators about Mengel's strange appearance. Besides an understandable weight loss from being on the run, Mengel's hair was closely cropped, he had no eyebrows, and was clean-shaven. More shockingly, he wore red lipstick.

Tranquada stated that he had asked Mengel about the lipstick. Mengel replied that his lips had become chapped from being out in the elements for days. Since he had no ChapStick available to him he used lipstick that he found in the car.

Tranquada further informed detectives that he and Mengel had driven to a nearby strip mall where Tranquada withdrew $300 from an ATM and gave the money to Mengel. Along with the cash, Tranquada volunteered that he also supplied Mengel with a pair of tennis shoes, socks, and gloves.

When pressed by detectives for Mengel's possible destination, Tranquada said Mengel told him that he was headed for Canada, most likely Toronto.

Detectives then asked him why he had not called police regarding Mengel. Tranquada simply answered that he didn't want to get involved. The young man was wrong as he was now involved up to his neck having committed a serious felony in providing the cop killer, Mengel, with money and clothes.

Buffalo detectives called the task force and informed them about Tranquada's statements regarding his aid to Mengel. In turn, Roach immediately apprised ADA Bendish of the situation and how this acquaintance of Mengel had clearly hindered his capture and prosecution.

Bendish wasted no time and personally dialed up Buffalo Homicide; within seconds, he was on the line with Tranquada. The veteran homicide prosecutor offered Tranquada immunity from prosecution, as long as he furnished detectives with a detailed sworn statement regarding his contact with Mengel and agreed to testify against him at trial.

Tranquada agreed quickly, but Bendish wasn't finished. Bendish's voice took on a steely cautionary tone as he informed Tranquada that if he withheld any information regarding his recent interaction with Mengel, or any information whatsoever, that he would undoubtedly finish his formal education inside the walls of a New York State prison.

Two lengthy and detailed sworn statements were taken from the university student regarding his meeting with Mengel. A Buffalo Homicide detective read the statements over the phone as Patalano, DeRosa and other task force detectives listened intently gathered around a speaker phone.

Chills ran up the backs of the detectives present when the Buffalo

Homicide detective read Tranquada's description of the car that Mengel operated; a new white Toyota, four-door sedan that was mud-covered. Tranquada was also observant enough to note that the vehicle's odometer read 1,200 miles and that a woman's handbag and assorted clothing was visible in the backseat of the vehicle.

Though neither the WCDPS nor Yonkers PD was directly involved in the missing person investigation of Beverly Capone, it was a major story that everyone in the county was well aware of.

Patalano immediately put out two APB notifications to alert every police agency in the northeast as well as Canada: the first, that Beverly Capone's missing Toyota Tercel, was quite possibly being operated by the cop killer, Alex J. Mengel and the second, to attempt to locate all recently stolen new or late model white Toyota four-door sedans.

16

On the evening of March 1, Beverly Capone's family and ex-husband, William, desperate to glean any information regarding her disappearance, now 96 hours old, placed a phone call to a well-known Westchester psychic, Carol Jayson.

In 1983, Ms. Jayson assisted White Plains Police in locating a young boy who had been kidnapped by his estranged father.

A skeptical William Capone asked Jayson if he could bring police detectives with him for a consultation on Saturday morning, March 2. Jayson accepted the request.

William Capone along with his daughter, Pamela, and no fewer than five police detectives were welcomed into Ms. Jayson's Yonkers apartment at 10 a.m., approximately the same time Troy Tranquada arrived at Buffalo Police Headquarters.

William Capone immediately pressed Jayson about Beverly's disappearance as the five detectives, three from Mount Vernon and two from the Dobbs Ferry Police Department, observed silently.

The psychic was silent as she appeared to attempt to process the questions and to gather impressions. *"There's more to it than just a missing person's case,"* Jayson responded with utter conviction. Her statement silenced the assembled group but Jayson wasn't near done yet.

"It has something to do with the name Prescott. I keep hearing Prescott… Prescott Street."

Though Prescott Street held absolutely no meaning for the Capone family or any recognizable lead for the Mount Vernon detectives, it clearly resonated with one of the Dobbs Ferry investigators, who continued to listen in silence.

"It's definitely Prescott Street," the psychic continued.

"Prescott Street is where the slain county police officer was found on Sunday night," the investigator informed.

Though terrified at the prospect of her mother having been taken by the cop killer, Pamela Capone was undeterred and queried Jayson, *"Do you see her car and is she in it?"*

"No," the psychic answered plainly.

"Where do you think her car might be?" William Capone followed up.

"Over the Tappan Zee Bridge. I see the bridge, but it's much farther

north...Haines Falls."

Haines Falls is a resort community in the Catskills, just a fifteen-minute drive from the Cairo/East Durham area. The Tappan Zee Bridge crosses the Hudson River and connects to the interstate which leads to the Catskill Region.

When the session ended, Ms. Jayson had not made any further connection to Gary's murder.

17

March 2, 1985, 4:46 p.m.
Scarborough, Canada

The Town of Scarborough is a bustling suburban community, a microcosm of the city that it borders, Toronto. The third shift of constables from the 41st Division of the Toronto Metropolitan Police had been on the street for about half an hour following their station house muster. During the muster, the lawmen were given a detailed briefing on the cop killer and suspected kidnapper, Mengel, who in all probability was headed directly to the city and suburbs they were charged with safeguarding.

Constable Clive Richards, 33, an eight-year veteran of the constabulary, began to canvass his sector known as 'The Golden Mile,' one of Canada's first industrial parks that was patterned after London's Golden Mile.

Richards knew that once you started searching for a particular make and color of car they seemed to abound. What he also understood was the best way for a fugitive to hide was in plain sight. Consequently, Richards turned his patrol car into the massive parking lot of the always-bustling Golden Mile Mall located at the intersection of Eglinton and Victoria Park Avenues.

The serious minded constable slowly perused the numerous rows of seemingly infinite parking spaces, keying in on any small white Toyotas. To the legion of shoppers, Richards appeared to be casually patrolling for "lawbreakers" like those who illegally park in handicapped spaces; that perception was fine with Richards.

The constable scanned ahead as he entered every new aisle and continued to do battle with the ubiquitous snow mounds, courtesy of a bitter winter, they impeded his view at nearly every turn. Undeterred, he craned his neck and looked left then right and back again combing the endless rows of cars.

Richards turned into the next isle and there it was. A new white Toyota Tercel facing out and idling in the shadow of one of the snow heaps. Remarkably, its assigned New York State registration plate 839TAI was still affixed. More exhilarating for Constable Richards was the fact that there was actually someone behind the wheel, a man. Richards knew it was

Alex Mengel.

Surrealism never entered Richards's mind as the predator, Mengel, stared knowingly back at him. Police work is often characterized as 95 percent boredom and five percent sheer terror and Richards was more than up for the challenge. Undaunted, he keyed his radio microphone and calmly requested back-up, all the while never once taking his eyes off the cop killer, who sat statue-like.

Alone and with total disregard for his own safety, Richards sprang out from his vehicle and into the open, drawing his weapon as he did so. With a two-handed combat grip, he leveled his sidearm at Mengel through the Toyota's windshield. Mengel, unmoved, considered his options briefly before flooring the gas pedal and catapulting the Toyota out from the space, just missing the constable's vehicle.

Richards leapt back into his patrol car and gave chase while advising headquarters of the pursuit. Richards knew exactly who he was dealing with, but Mengel had no idea just who this courageous constable was. This was Richards's fourth job in law enforcement, and he had dealt with the scum like he now chased in the slums of Hong Kong and in the Rookeries of London's East End.

Two marked units quickly joined Richards in the high-speed pursuit of Mengel westbound on Eglinton Avenue. The pursuing officers had a myriad of dangerous factors to consider; though it was a weekend, it surely was rush hour in this commercial area. More distressing, would the murderer and kidnapper attempt to take a hostage or shoot it out with police, further endangering civilian lives, if he was cornered?

Mengel weaved the Toyota in and out of the heavily-congested roadway and turned right onto Sloane Avenue. Richards was right on his bumper and realized that, when Mengel did come to a stop, he would have to soundly put an end to this fugitive's run one way or another and most likely with deadly force.

Mengel saw the red light up ahead and that all three lanes of traffic were densely packed with stopped motorists. He turned the stolen Toyota hard right towards the parking lot of a car dealership. A thin sheet of ice caused the Toyota to careen sideways out of control, crashing into a sign pole encased in a snow bank.

Mengel bailed out of the vehicle and fled towards the dealership's showroom that teemed with people. Richards raced after him with gun in hand. Mengel, at a half trot, turned sideways toward the pursuing constable as he pulled something from his waistband, a handgun. Mengel nearly fumbled the weapon and struggled to gain control of it. Richards stopped and took up a defensive posture, his gun up and pointed at the still-moving Mengel. Richards eased the slack from his revolver's trigger.

A microsecond later, the handgun that Mengel juggled fell to the pavement. A stainless steel revolver glistened in the evening light against the icy black top. Later it would be identified as Gary Stymiloski's service revolver.

Mengel's inadvertent slip-up surely saved his life as the veteran lawman Richards, who would have been totally justified in the use of deadly force, showed remarkable restraint in not firing on Mengel. It was obvious that Mengel intended to murder another law enforcement officer to insure his escape.

With his weapon-trained center mass on a now-surrendering Mengel, Richards warned his fellow officers about the discarded weapon as Mengel raised his hands above his head. Then Constables Peter Howorth and Herbert Lawrence held Mengel at gunpoint as Constable Clive Richards placed the 'most wanted' man in North America in handcuffs and under arrest.

18

At 8:10 p.m., just over two hours after being informed of Mengel's capture, DeRosa, Patalano, Roach and task force commanders McClain and Sweeney boarded American Airlines Flight 122 from LaGuardia Airport to Toronto. The task force, though exhilarated by Mengel's capture, knew there was still no sign of Beverly Capone and the probability of finding her alive was becoming less likely by the minute.

Near midnight, the task force was given a briefing on the arrest of Alex J. Mengel at the 41st Division in Toronto. Toronto detectives informed that the weapon that Mengel had dropped matched the serial number of Gary's department issue revolver. Additionally, they informed that a second handgun, a Star .380 semi-automatic pistol, was later recovered from the Toyota.

The American police were overjoyed. They now had the murder weapon used to kill Gary and Gary's missing service weapon in Mengel's possession, along with the three eyewitness statements from Mohan, Jardine and Ramroop. Mengel was done.

Now the task force wanted to know about Capone. Besides her car, was there any other sign or evidence of her? Toronto investigators stated that Beverly Capone's New York State driver's license was found on Mengel's person and that it had been altered with Mengel's photo likeness covering Capone's photo, though everything else appeared the same. The information momentarily puzzled the task force, but the Canadian officials weren't done yet.

They advised there was something else recovered from the Toyota, something horrific and evidently human: a scalp. The discovery was made under the driver's seat and was first thought by police to be a wig. Upon closer examination of the longish dark-haired "wig," both skin tissue and dried blood were present. The grisly evidence was in the process of being sent to the Toronto Police crime lab for testing.

The bizarre find staggered the New York investigators. The numerous interviews that DeRosa and Patalano conducted with Mengel's friends and associates flashed into both investigators' minds as they recalled how Mengel was consistently depicted as a skilled hunter who regularly skinned his prey. Days later, Phywreen Mengel recounted how some time ago, Mengel insisted that she view a video of what seemed to be autopsies.

Now the attempted abduction of the Skaneateles paper girl by the man identified as Mengel disguised as a woman, wearing an ill-fitting wig made all the more sense, though in a maddening way.

The Toronto investigators added that, when they queried Mengel about Capone, he said he had no knowledge of any woman and that he had come upon the Toyota Tercel by the "*big lake*." Mengel admitted to stealing the vehicle after picking the lock and finding the ignition key inside a woman's handbag that also contained Beverly Capone's license.

With the Canadian's blessings, task force members agreed to wait and interview Mengel the next afternoon. Over the next twelve hours, the American detectives hoped to devise a 'Hail Mary' strategy to obtain a statement from Mengel in regards to his involvement with Capone's disappearance; that would cause him to waive his rights to an extradition hearing.

DeRosa's night, however, wasn't over yet; he wanted to see Capone's recovered Toyota. The car was unsealed by evidence technicians and DeRosa studied the mud-covered vehicle from the outside. He inquired about the front passenger door; was it operational from the inside? The evidence tech, his curiosity piqued at the question, checked the functionality of the door handle. The door failed to open from the inside, just like Mengel's *Ghostbusters* Capri.

Beverly Capone's 1985 Toyota inside the
Toronto Police evidence facility.

By mid-morning on Sunday March 3rd, the task force convened in their hotel's lobby over a large breakfast. Roach, who undoubtedly believed that Mengel would never waive his right to extradition, had just returned from viewing Capone's Toyota and there was something that didn't fit: a weathered and stained comforter in the backseat.

DeRosa commented that he viewed the item in the same way and found it unlikely that the elegant Capone would have such an item in her brand new car. The comforter had to have been put there by Mengel. Seconds later, DeRosa was on the phone with Pamela Capone. She had no recollection of such an article of bedding in her mother's car or apartment.

After DeRosa informed his colleagues of his conversation with Pamela, Roach recalled that Mengel's friend Singh, in one of his interviews, spoke of an abandoned shed at the East Durham campsite. Singh said Mengel used to store camping equipment there, and, at times, slept there when he couldn't afford a motel room.

Mengel had to have been there at that campsite and obviously brought Beverly with him. But where was Beverly now?

Out of deference to the WCDPS, it was decided that DeRosa, and Deputy Commissioner Sweeney speak with Mengel first. The two officials entered the interview room where Mengel sat chained to a desk. DeRosa and Sweeney identified themselves to Mengel and then immediately asked him where and when he had obtained the white Toyota.

Mengel repeated what he had told Toronto Police, that he found the car in a parking lot by the big lake on Wednesday evening around dusk. DeRosa, like any detective worth his salt, already knew the answer to his next question and simply wanted to get a baseline of Mengel's truthfulness to a non-incriminating question.

Mengel replied no that he didn't think so when asked if he had been to the big lake before. DeRosa countered that Mengel's friend Singh stated he, Mengel, and Mohan had fished the waters there many times.

Mengel considered DeRosa's comment and replied that it was possible but that his *"head was not working right."*

DeRosa and Sweeney queried Mengel on his whereabouts after he abandoned "Sam-One" and the next day. Mengel said that he had stayed in a shack by the *"big hotel"* and then walked north along the east side of the parkway till late on Monday night, before sleeping next to a makeshift fire.

Mengel recounted how he stole the white Toyota and drove very fast, *"over ninety miles an hour"* up the Saw Mill River Parkway then onto the Taconic State Parkway and arrived in the Cairo area, simply to make a phone call to Tranquada. Mengel then foolishly added that he was in the area for only minutes and then headed to Buffalo.

DeRosa sensed his opportunity and pounced; *"When did you pick up the comforter from the shed?"*

Mengel was momentarily taken aback as his mind raced on how the police had connected the comforter to him. He then adamantly denied that he had been to that location at all and that the comforter had been in the

Toyota when he entered it.

Minutes later, Roach, Patalano and McClain now sat before Mengel. Patalano asked Mengel if he would waive his right to an extradition hearing and return with them to the US. Mengel replied no, he would not.

"Do you know the whereabouts of the missing woman, Beverly Capone?" McClain asked Mengel.

Mengel emphatically denied any knowledge of Beverly and appeared on the verge of tears as he further added, *"Had there been a woman around the car, I would not have taken it."*

Mengel was asked two additional times if he would waive his right to an extradition hearing; he responded negatively both times.

South of the border, back in Westchester County, DA Carl A. Vergari, who held the post for a remarkable 25 years, transforming the office into a first rate prosecutorial organization stood before Judge James R. Cowhey, in county criminal court. Vergari wasn't alone. Mengel associates, Raymond Jardine and Gloria Ramroop, their secrets finally uncovered, stood nearby as did ADA Bendish.

WCDPS Narcotics Detective Paul Geiger, whose involvement in the investigation of Gary's murder was strictly peripheral, learned through a confidential informant that Jardine was illegally in the United States. Soon after, Ramroop's illegal status was also exposed, following claims that her US Passport had been stolen.

Vergari made his argument to the court that both Jardine and Ramroop, eyewitnesses to Officer Stymiloski's murder should be classified as material witnesses; as these associates of Mengel *"weren't likely to be around when a trial commenced."* Judge Cowhey concurred and set bail for the couple. Unable to raise the sum, Jardine and Ramroop found themselves in protective custody at the Westchester County Jail in Valhalla.

Vergari, when pressed by reporters about the couple's incarceration stated, *"They will be held as long as it's necessary to conclude this case."*

19

On March 4, Mengel sat in a cell at the Toronto East Detention Center, a maximum security jail, on three charges of illegal weapons possession. Just blocks away at the Centre for Forensic Sciences, scientists and technicians were in the initial stages of comparison testing between the recovered human scalp and hair brushes used by Beverly Capone that were provided by her daughter.

Back in Westchester County, DA Carl Vergari and Homicide Bureau Chief Bendish prepared their case with task force detectives for presentation to a grand jury to secure a first-degree murder indictment of Mengel.

Newspapers in New York and Canada were reporting on just how Mengel entered the country. Unidentified Canadian law enforcement officials said it was clear that Mengel crossed the border disguised as a woman in Beverly Capone's Toyota. Officials also reported that he altered the photo on Capone's New York State driver's license and presented it to border officials to gain entrance, a scenario that, if proven true, were clear violations of Canadian Immigration Law.

Behind the scenes, unidentified friends of Mengel were in the process of hiring well-known civil rights attorney Michael Smith to represent him. Smith was known as the 'Canadian William Kunstler' and all of his fees would be paid by Canadian taxpayers.

Though the majority of interest involving the case was concentrated north of the US border, a New York State Police crime scene unit arrived at the burglarized cabin in East Durham some three days after Roach's request.

As one crime scene investigator dusted the glass of the sliding door and its handle for prints, another began his search of the cabin's lone bedroom.

The investigator combed through the sparse contents of drawers contained in the modest bureau. Upon sliding open the bottom drawer, there was what looked like an ID card. The card was face up and contained a photo of a woman who stared up unafraid. It was an IBM employee identification card issued to Beverly Capone.

The card and its placement proved definitively that the still-unaccounted-for Beverly Capone, had been in the cabin. She bravely secreted her ID card there. It was the only piece of evidence that Beverly could leave behind proving that she had been there against her will. It also indicated to the task force that Beverly had resigned herself to the fact that the monster, Mengel., would end her life.

The crucial find sent shockwaves through the now embarrassed state police hierarchy as their agency appeared complacent and incompetent.

When the initial request for a state police crime scene unit was made, cop killer Mengel was still on the run. Due to the state's lackluster response, another 72 hours of not knowing what had become of their loved one passed painfully for Beverly's family.

The owners of the cabin, the Metz Family, a married couple from New Jersey, were requested by authorities to immediately come to their property in hope that they could shed some light on anything in the cabin that didn't belong there or was missing.

Upon arrival the couple was asked to supply fingerprint samples and blood types so they could be ruled out.

Shortly thereafter, specks of blood, along with several latent fingerprints, were recovered from inside the cabin's bedroom and bathroom. Ultimately, these were positively identified as Beverly Capone's. Mrs. Metz noted that several things were amiss in her ransacked summer cabin. In particular, an old house coat was missing, along with the bathroom shower curtain.

In response, the state police conducted a renewed search of the woods through East Durham and Cairo, doubling their resources to include scuba divers and twenty Rangers from the US Park Service.

Later that evening back in Toronto, an observant detention officer noticed that the lighting in Mengel's cell appeared dimmer than usual. Several officers entered the cell to find that Mengel had dismantled a security light fixture and secreted several pieces of metal from the fixture on his person. Mengel had no physical signs that he had attempted to harm himself with the items but was charged with damaging government property.

Though Mengel denied the accusation, Superintendent Peter Jackson stated, *"It's certainly suspicious behavior and a building security concern."*

In one of Mohan's detailed statements, he recalled how Mengel regularly enjoyed putting people in handcuffs and, though he had no key for them, he would use a metal shim to open them.

On Monday, March 11, Mengel, who repeatedly refused to waive extradition to the US by remaining silent and refusing to testify, appeared at a deportation hearing with his new legal counsel, Michael Smith. Smith argued that Mengel, in fact, *"had legal visitor status"* in Canada. Under Canadian Immigration Law, an émigré may be deported if found that he entered the country under fraudulent means or that he entered the country without the means to support himself.

Smith's play was to gain refugee status for Mengel, virtually ending any possibility of deportation. This would force Canadian and US law enforcement to pursue a more difficult and lengthier extradition proceeding.

Under international law, refugee status may be granted to an applicant who proves that he fears persecution upon his return to another country because of race, religion, nationality, membership in a particular social group, or political opinion. Ironically, the US had issued legal alien status and all the protections it afforded to the man who now sought refugee status in Canada.

After the hearing, Smith told reporters, *"They say they are trying to deport him because of an alleged illegal entry. But we know the primary reasons they are interested is because of the murder of a police officer and the disappearance of a woman."*

Over the next ten days following the recovery of Capone's ID card, state police officials released the following quotes to the media: *"Basically, we can't say for sure that she was here. We're going to cut the search back somewhat . . . It's not likely we will find her here, the leads are winding down."*

Is missing woman victim of cop killer?

Beverly Capone, 44, of Mount Vernon, who was reported missing

20

Robert Langendoen was curious about the incoming phone message regarding Beverly Capone, recording on his home answering machine on that February afternoon in 2013. Intrigued, Langendoen lifted the receiver and spoke softly. *"I remember it like it was yesterday, the Ides of March."*

Langendoen, 58, is considered an international expert in the use of scent dogs for search-and-rescue purposes. His record is stellar, having never once had any other handler make a "find" in an area that he pronounced cleared.

Langendoen's searches run the gamut from the garden variety, lost children and Alzheimer patients to the dangerous, hunting armed criminals to the exotic, locating bones from the 17th century in swamp waters to his most celebrated and tragic, find, Beverly Capone.

Langendoen is mild-mannered and treats his veteran scent dog, Micah, and young recruit, Cayce, like a doting father treats his children. On June 1, 2013, in East Durham, he graciously reenacted his search efforts and ultimate discovery of Beverly Capone's body nearly 30 years in the past.

Langendoen with his trademark White German Shepherds, Micah, foreground and Cayce.

Langendoen and Cayce.

On the day of the original search for Beverly Capone, Langendoen and Flash started in the cabin's bedroom. Flash sniffed the bed's sheets for Beverly's scent, the location where most of the blood had been recovered from. The duo then tracked north into the woods.

"We had two teams that day and I had made several passes with Flash over four hours in our sector. As we traversed along the Catskill Creek, Flash was definitely picking up a scent, so we continued along the water line. Then it seemed like he lost the scent. I then realized that the scent he initially sensed must have been coming from above us on the high ground and we started up the hill."

Though Langendoen, modest to a fault, never offers the fact that the dog is only as good as the handler, insiders know it is the foundation for any successful K-9 team. The work ethic of the handler and his own powers of detection is the difference between consistent finds and failure.

"Once we were on the high ground, Flash definitely found something. Exactly what, I wasn't sure. The landscape in the area was denoted by a series of three-foot-high fieldstone walls that were each well over a hundred years old."

"Then I saw that there were several missing stones from one wall. I wondered why someone had removed them; maybe a child had done it. We moved around the immediate area and then I saw the missing stones. They were easily recognizable due to their underside color that hadn't been directly exposed to the elements. The stones had been placed alongside another fieldstone wall and definitely didn't belong there. I knew then that we had found Miss Capone."

The believed recovery site of Beverly Capone's body on March 15, 1985

Beverly Capone's body was officially recovered by state police investigators some hours later, clad in a housecoat and wrapped in a shower curtain; the same two items reported missing by Mrs. Metz.

Ironically, a Catholic of great faith, Beverly's remains were located approximately 200 yards from Our Lady of Knock Shrine on Route 145. The story of Knock started on August 21, 1879, when, at approximately eight o'clock in the evening, fifteen people from the Village of Knock, in County Mayo, Ireland, witnessed an apparition of Our Lady, St. Joseph, St. John the Evangelist and a lamb on an altar with a cross at the gable wall of the parish church. The witnesses watched the apparition in the pouring rain for two hours, reciting the Rosary.

Although they, themselves, were saturated, not a single drop of rain fell on the gable or vision. Most of the fifteen official witnesses were from the Village of Knock or surrounding area and ranged in age from just five years old to 74 years old. Each of the witnesses gave testimonies to a Commission of Inquiry held in October 1879. The findings of the Commission were that the testimonies were both trustworthy and satisfactory.

Our Lady of Knock Shrine Church on Rte. 145 in East Durham.

Beverly's sister, Tina Knapp, issued a statement to the press that evening on behalf of the family. *"I would like to thank all the law enforcement agencies and others involved in the case. Pamela, Billy [William] and I will never forget the special kindness we received from our own Mount Vernon Police Department. As far as Mengel is concerned, we'll leave that up to the courts and God."*

21

"Oh Lord, you sweep men away like a dream. Like grass that springs up in the morning and by evening it withers and dies." Those words, excerpts from the 90th Psalm of the Old Testament spoken by the Reverend Nicholas Basile, echoed throughout St. Francis of Assisi Church in Mount Vernon on the first day of spring, March 20, 1985.

A blue casket bearing the body of Beverly Capone was perched in the aisle near her daughter Pamela, sister Tina Knapp, and former husband William Capone. Numerous extended family members and friends, along with county and local officials, filled the rest of the church.

Too distraught to read a last address to her mother, Pamela Capone's cousin, Carl Kiefer, eloquently did so. *"Mom, there are so many things I wanted to tell you, but time and circumstances have taken that away from us now. For now, I pray for the day when we are again in God's kingdom."*

Following the one-hour Mass, a 30-car motorcade passed through the streets of Mount Vernon to include Beverly's residence on its way to the Beechwoods Cemetery in New Rochelle.

Family member Frank D'Agostino said that the family wanted to forget the circumstances regarding Mrs. Capone's death. *"We just want to lay Beverly to rest with dignity."*

And so she was. Beverly Capone had, in fact, lived a most dignified life, having faced and overcome a plethora of hardships and heartache. Though small in stature, her spirit and zest for life was unmatched.

Before entering her teenage years, Beverly learned just how harsh the world could be. The eldest of eight children, her parents ended their marriage and their family, as they placed all of their children in foster care, some in homes far across the country. Beverly and her sister Tina wound up in Mount Vernon.

Married after graduating from Evander Childs High School in the Bronx, the whirlwind young courtship didn't last, but produced her pride and joy, Pamela. Possessed with a burning passion to succeed in the world, Beverly worked hard to support herself and her daughter.

Tragedy would strike Beverly again in 1970 when she was informed that her natural mother had been stabbed to death.

Undaunted, a dedicated and savvy Beverly constantly strived to improve herself by taking computer courses and reading self-help books.

During this time she even took in one of her younger brothers, Robert, while he finished high school.

Beverly's hard work paid off, attaining a data processing position at the Mount Vernon Board of Education. That position lasted for over ten years, along with part-time work with the city's police department before moving onto IBM.

In a local newspaper interview, close friend and neighbor Elizabeth DeMarco said, *"Beverly was content in her life and the little things pleased her. She was very proud of Pamela, who was pursuing a career in clothing design, and of her own promotion at IBM."* DeMarco went on to say, *"In fact, we talked about putting curtains up in her new office just last week; she couldn't wait to get in and decorate."*

Beverly was also an avid reader. In the same newspaper interview, co-worker and close friend Marie Austin recalled how Beverly had introduced her to books such as *Jonathan Livingston Seagull* and *The Magic of Thinking Big*.

Ms. Austin also produced another gift from Beverly — a laminated card bearing the Prayer to St. Jude, the patron saint of lost hope. *"She was always praying to St. Jude,"* Austin informed.

22

On Tuesday, March 26, Westchester residents awoke to the news that Mengel's hearing on illegal weapons possession had been postponed for a third time. This time, though, it was for a promising reason: a pending deportation ruling that could come within hours.

Though Canadian Justice and Immigration officials publically maintained their impartiality and followed the law to the letter, the horrendous developments surrounding Mengel's case privately sickened them.

Back in Greene County in New York, District Attorney Seymour Meadow began impaneling a grand jury that he intended to present a second-degree murder charge to against Mengel. Meadow, one week earlier armed with Beverly Capone's autopsy report along with a myriad of other evidence implicating Mengel, easily secured a warrant for his arrest. The autopsy report found that Beverly Capone's cause of death was from two stab wounds to her upper left chest. It also contained other grisly post mortem details that investigators believed they already knew. Beverly Capone was in fact, scalped, and her face had been crudely Degloved by a sharp instrument. It was a consensus among task force members that Mengel planned to use the devitalized facial tissue as a further disguise, but it had failed, due to his bone structure.

At mid-morning inside the Westchester County Office and Courthouse building in White Plains, the grand jury impaneled there to hear the case against Mengel heard testimony from a very special witness, Toronto Constable Clive Richards. Richards calmly answered ADA Bendish's questions and recounted his dramatic confrontation and subsequent arrest of Mengel to a riveted panel of 26 jurors.

After his testimony, Richards, whose legendary status and celebrity in the law enforcement community and beyond was building by the minute, was escorted upstairs to Westchester County Executive Andrew P. O'Rourke's office. A twenty-minute ceremony followed commemorating the constable's heroic actions.

Richards was presented with a plaque by O'Rourke and Mosca from the WCDPS, thanking him and his fellow officers from the 41st Division. He also received numerous letters of appreciation, including one from O'Rourke and the WCDPS PBA as his beaming wife, Wendy, looked on.

Richards said he was *"overwhelmed by the great treatment he had received"* ... hoped to see a bit of New York City ... *"it's a pity that we had to come together in this manner."*

Later, Richards spoke publically about his arrest of Mengel with reporters: *"It was a bit scary, but you don't think too much about it at the time. I was going to make that arrest no matter what it took."*

At approximately 11:30 a.m. local time, after an hour of evidence summation by Canadian immigration enforcement officials against Mengel, Adjudicator J.D. Benning ruled that Mengel entered Canada illegally by using the altered New York driver's license of Beverly Capone. Mengel stood next to his attorney impassively as Adjudicator Benning spoke directly to him. *"Mister Mengel, you are to be deported to the United States of America as soon as practicable."*

The promising news was immediately communicated to task force detectives in Westchester. Yet there was still one possible caveat; Mengel did have the right under Canadian Immigration Law to appeal the ruling within 24 hours. Such an appeal could take as long as another 30 days to resolve.

Law enforcement on both sides of the border waited with baited breath over the next 24 hours to see if Mengel's attorney would appeal the decision.

On Wednesday morning, Mengel's attorney decided against appealing his client's immigration case and the Canadian 'wheels of justice' went into high speed. Deputy Crown Attorney Kenneth Anthony, who had formally charged Mengel with the illegal weapons possession, moved to withdraw the charges. Ontario Provincial Court Judge Gordon Tinker immediately approved the request at an 11 a.m. hearing.

Canadian immigration officials then drove Mengel to the Lewiston-Queenston Bridge at the US-Canadian border near Niagara Falls where DeRosa and Patalano waited patiently. Though stone-faced, both detectives relished the moment to finally and officially arrest Mengel for Gary's murder.

As soon as the Canadian official's handcuffs were removed from Mengel, DeRosa firmly replaced them with one of the two pairs that he always carried as his partner, Patalano, read Mengel his rights from a laminated Miranda Warnings card. Mengel stayed silent, never once answering Patalano's prompts in regards to understanding his rights.

With DeRosa and Patalano on either side of Mengel in the back of a Buffalo police cruiser, they were whisked to Buffalo International Airport and boarded a US Air flight bound for LaGuardia Airport.

DeRosa was later quoted in newspapers regarding Mengel during the flight. *"He just sat there and said and did absolutely nothing."*

Upon landing at the airport in New York City, Mengel was hustled into one of four WCDPS patrol cars, whose emergency lights were flashing. The four patrol cars were sandwiched between two NYPD Highway Patrol cruisers that escorted the Westchester contingent in emergency mode over the Whitestone Bridge onto the Hutchinson River Parkway and up to the Bronx-Westchester border.

The four WCDPS patrol cars, three of which contained four officers each, raced up to the front of the WCDPS headquarters in Hawthorne at approximately 4:30 p.m. A small army of police personnel, all wearing black armbands, looked on, as a front-cuffed Mengel, exited a patrol car. Flanked by DeRosa and Patalano, Mengel was guided quickly up the slate walkway.

Mengel back in N.Y. on murder charge

By Kevin McCoy
and Will David
Staff Writers

Ending more than three weeks of legal and immigration battles in Canada, the accused murderer of a Westchester County police officer and a Mount Vernon woman returned to New York Wednesday to face prosecution.

Alexander J. Mengel, a 30-year-old Guyana native, walked beneath a flag lowered to half-staff at Westchester County Police headquarters in Hawthorne and formally was charged with first-degree murder in the Feb. 24 shooting of Officer Gary Styznikski.

The Bronx resident, transferred from Toronto to New York Wednesday under heavy police security, offered only brief, barely audible replies to identification queries from Westchester County Police Lt. John Calvert during a brief booking procedure.

After the booking, police whisked Mengel to Yonkers Criminal Court, where Judge Bruce Tolbert arraigned him on the murder charge and ordered the suspect held without bail at the Westchester County Jail in Valhalla.

Claire Palermo, a Westchester County spokeswoman, said Mengel would be held under a constant suicide watch in a partially segregated security section of the jail.

Assistant Westchester District Attorney Bruce Bendish said he expected a county grand jury — which is scheduled to hear testimony from Metropolitan Toronto Police Constable Clive Richards this morning — to indict Mengel for the

Mengel cowered at the impressive show of force and overwhelming solidarity. He never once raised his head but his eyes clearly scanned up at the United States and Westchester County flags that sat at half-mast along with the black bunting that draped the building's facade. An impressive plaque of a police badge carved from wood was affixed just above the front entrance. It read 'MEMORIAL IN MEMORY OF OUR ILLUSTRIOUS DEAD Westchester County Police.'

Mosca, who waited at the top of the stairs, glared at Mengel before he entered the building to be 'booked' for the murder of Gary by the officer-in-charge, Lieutenant John Calvert.

Mosca later addressed reporters during a brief press conference. *"I think we should've had the death penalty ten years ago. Now let the punishment fit the crimes."*

Mengel's day was by no means over as he was then caravanned to Yonkers Criminal Court in downtown Yonkers for arraignment on murder and a myriad of other charges. At 5:15 p.m., Mengel with his new counsel, John Ryan, at his side, stood before 37 year-old Judge Bruce Tolbert, the first African-American Republican Judge in Yonkers History. Homicide prosecutor Bendish was poised nearby.

Judge Tolbert addressed Mengel, *"Are you Alex Mengel?"* Mengel nodded once. Tolbert advised him of his rights as a defendant and remanded him to the Westchester County Jail without bail. Mengel never spoke a word or made another gesture.

At 6 p.m., DeRosa and Patalano's whirlwind day was finally over as they transferred Mengel to the custody of Westchester County correction officials in Valhalla.

Years later, DeRosa spoke about that day: *"It was the most important arrest of my career."*

Now twice a grandfather, he appears as fit today as on that March day some 30 years ago. DeRosa recalled a private moment that night, with his then ten year-old daughter, Kristy, who had a question; *"Why did he kill Gary?"*

DeRosa's reply, *"Even God doesn't know."*

It's obvious that DeRosa, still bears the emotional scars of the senseless and barbaric violence that claimed Gary and Beverly's young lives.

But then DeRosa, shakes off the cold memory and flashes a wide smile of befuddlement, as he points to that famous front page newspaper picture of him and Patalano, ushering Mengel, into headquarters. *"I can't believe I wore that checkered shirt, on such an important day."*

23

Within 24 hours of Mengel's return to Westchester County, the grand jury, considering the charges against him, returned a 'true bill,' finding sufficient cause to pursue all the charges and indict him.

As in all felony cases, the Westchester County Court in White Plains had exclusive authority to try Mengel. On April 8, a handcuffed Mengel, shackled and surrounded by court officers, stood before Judge Nicholas Colabella as a packed courtroom looked on. Mengel's lawyer, John Ryan, entered a plea of not guilty to all eleven charges ranging from driving without a license through first-degree robbery, to first-degree murder of Police Officer Gary Stymiloski.

Ryan did not seek bail and following the ten-minute proceeding, Mengel was returned to the county jail in Valhalla. Over the next seventeen days, Homicide Chief Bendish and his boss, DA Vagari, though confident that their case against Mengel was iron-clad; worked feverishly to make their prosecution as error-free as possible and prepared for Mengel's only possible defense — insanity.

New York State politics now entered the case as the state no longer had the death penalty for first-degree murder, not even for a law enforcement officer in the performance of his duties. After Mengel's deportation, the state assembly in Albany passed a death penalty bill only to be summarily vetoed by then Democratic Governor Mario M. Cuomo.

Meanwhile, Mengel had another high-profile murder to answer for: Beverly Capone's. On the morning of April 26, BCI Senior Investigator, Fred Grunwald, who had searched with task force detectives for Mengel upstate, arrived at the Westchester County Jail with his partner, Robert Stabile. These state investigators were assigned to transport Mengel to his arraignment some 90 miles away in the Village of Catskill.

Accustomed to run-of-the-mill DWIs and petty theft cases, Main Street was lined with onlookers, reporters, and TV cameras as the alleged double murderer, Mengel, arrived at the courthouse that day.

Village public defender Greg Lebow was appointed to be Mengel's attorney. Lebow, now in private practice just doors down from the courthouse recalled that day; *"I met with him in a holding area under the courthouse while he ate lunch. He didn't seem to be too engaged but we did discuss his defense for about twenty minutes or so. It was just after one when we stepped into the courtroom for his arraignment. The whole process was less than twenty minutes as I entered a not guilty plea on his behalf."*

After the proceeding, Mengel and his state police escort started back to Westchester in the unmarked Chevy Celebrity sedan. Mengel was secured with front-cuffed hands attached to a heavy steel chain around his midsection, along with leg shackles. He was in the rear passenger seat next to Grunwald, who sat behind the driver, Stabile.

An hour later, a salesman from Westchester, who coincidentally bore the same name as Mengel's new attorney, John Ryan, was driving behind the vehicle that carried Mengel. Both cars travelled southbound on the Taconic State Parkway in the Town of Fishkill in Dutchess County.

Ryan, lost in thought, was whisked back into reality as a commotion erupted in the back seat of the vehicle ahead of him. Ryan had no idea that the vehicle was carrying Mengel and his state police escort. Ryan edged up in his seat; he clearly saw two figures struggling in the back seat.

Inside the unmarked vehicle, Mengel attacked Grunwald by slamming his head into the side of the lawman's face. The blow stunned Grunwald. Mengel continued the onslaught. Using his legs, Mengel leveraged his body weight, pinning the dazed investigator up against the door, all the while, reaching for the handgun strapped to Grunwald's right side.

Grunwald, his left side wedged against the door, tried to repel the attack with his right hand. Horrifyingly, he felt Mengel tugging at the holstered weapon. The investigator desperately grabbed for his weapon, only to find Mengel's hands already clutching its checkered wooden grips that jutted high out from its holster.

Grunwald clutched his right hand over Mengel's cuffed hands. Mengel countered like a caged animal. Viciously, he twice bit through the lawman's right shirt sleeve, causing open wounds on Grunwald's upper arm and shoulder.

Mengel wrenched the handgun free from the holster as Grunwald frantically battled for control of his weapon. Grunwald grasped the Magnum's steel frame just under the hammer and covered the trigger guard in hopes of keeping Mengel's trigger finger at bay.

The blitz attack on Grunwald was just seconds old when he called out to his partner, Stabile. *"Bob, he's going for my gun!"*

Meanwhile, Ryan sped up to get a closer look of exactly what was occurring in the backseat of the blue Chevy. Some 50 yards past Knapp Road, a wide-eyed Ryan slammed on his brakes as the Chevy broke hard right and came to a screeching halt, nearly striking the guardrail.

Once Stabile brought the vehicle to a complete stop, he acted swiftly. While whirling about in his seat, he simultaneously drew his Smith and Wesson .357 snub-nosed revolver.

He was taken aback upon seeing his partner bloodied and battered by

Mengel's frenzied and ongoing attack. Mengel just finished gnawing at Grunwald's flesh once more, this time higher up on his shoulder and dangerously close to his neck.

Stabile looked down at his partner's un-holstered handgun that the two men fought for control of and that was precariously pointed towards the front passenger compartment.

Mengel jerked forcefully away from Grunwald in hopes of completely wrenching the weapon from his hand. Remarkably, Grunwald's panicked grip was too strong for him. Undeterred, with his hands still firmly on the weapon's grips, Mengel continued to attempt to dislodge the weapon from the investigator's hand.

Mengel peered up at Stabile and the gun he wielded. Undaunted, he snarled at him, revealing bloodied teeth. He then began to turn back towards Grunwald to certainly once again tear at his flesh and this time gain total control of the handgun.

Stabile acted accordingly as any law enforcement officer would do when faced with a rabid attacking animal; he put him down. The single headshot soundly ended the brutal encounter and utter malevolent life of Alex J. Mengel.

Ryan had stopped his vehicle directly behind the unmarked Chevy. Though the sound of the gunshot was muffled by the car's interior, Ryan believed the report to be what it was and cautiously exited his car.

A shaken Stabile radioed for back up, an ambulance and supervision as both he and the injured Grunwald emerged from their vehicle and stood beside the open rear passenger door.

Unsure but believing the two men to be police officers, Ryan treaded lightly then asked if they needed help. A bloodied and thoroughly-drained Grunwald replied stoically, *"It's a state police matter."*

Ryan peered curiously through the open backseat door at the deceased Mengel. Blood from the gaping head wound flowed onto the floor mats.

Once several state police units arrived on scene, both investigators were rushed by troopers to the ER at St. Francis Hospital in the City of Poughkeepsie for trauma and Grunwald's multiple human bite wounds.

Shortly after Mengel was officially pronounced dead at the scene, his body was subsequently transferred to the Dutchess County's medical examiner's office.

Hours later, Stabile and Grunwald, lucky to be alive, were released from the hospital. The two investigators were now the second and third law enforcement officers in just two months to survive near deadly encounters with Mengel since he assassinated Gary.

24

"As clean as a white sheet…"

Hours after Mengel's death, task force detectives apprised both the Stymiloski and Capone families of the incident.

In the living room of her Yonkers home, Dorothy Stymiloski slowly rocked back and forth in a comfortable chair and repeated the same words in a barely audible voice. *"It's justice from the grave."*

From his fifth floor apartment in Mount Vernon, William Capone was somewhat relieved by the news but stated, *"He just should have suffered more. He made Beverly suffer so much."*

Dorothy Stymiloski, 59, and her husband, Edward Sr., 60, said Mengel *"surely would have killed again in police custody."*

Mrs. Stymiloski then stated, *"My son was just doing his job and he murdered him. Now justice has finally been done. Now the cries of the victims have been heard."*

There were a number of other comments and observations made as well. Subhas Singh, the man who knowingly and intentionally withheld vital information from police concerning Mengel that may have prevented Beverly Capone's murder stated, *"No police officer can tell me you transport the most dangerous criminal in the United States in a regular car. He should have been transported in a high security truck."*

Gustav Mengel observed, *"You don't just lead a dangerous bear around with just wire around his hands."*

Dangerous criminals are transported daily by law enforcement today in nearly the same fashion that Mengel was on that day. The main difference is a simple one: today, all prisoners are now mandated to be seat-belted in, mostly for obvious purposes, but it also clearly provides another layer of physical restraint.

In regards to front-cuffed prisoners, that procedure is for humanitarian purposes as prisoner transports can be lengthy, not only in miles but in wait time. Additionally, even if a police car is outfitted with a partition, the transporting officers are still responsible for the in-transit security and safety of that prisoner at all times.

Gustav Mengel made additional comments in regards to his brother's death: *"What happened there wasn't right. It was a case of police revenge. I want to find out exactly what happened to make them shoot him and kill him."*

On May 9, the Dutchess County grand jury impaneled to consider the circumstances of Mengel's death and the actions of Stabile and Grunwald delivered their findings to District Attorney William Grady. The jury, which consisted of 28 panelists, found the use of deadly force against Mengel justified and that no further legal action was warranted against either Stabile or Grunwald in regards to the matter.

Over a three-day period, the jury heard testimony from both state investigators, who did so without immunity, along with forensic crime scene experts and the only civilian eyewitness, John Ryan.

After learning of the decision, Stabile said, *"I think the evidence speaks for itself. You hope your training pays off at a time like that."*

In 1986, Stabile received his agency's highest award for heroism, the 'Brummer Award' for the actions he took on that April afternoon in 1985.

"The whole family has a record as clean as a white sheet." This statement was made by Gustav Mengel just days after his brother's capture in Canada.

Mengel further observed that his brother's alleged acts *"had ruined his family."* Mengel then followed with a curious comment: *"It ruined my life at work…I have people looking at me as if I were involved."* These statements made by Mengel provide some interesting insight into his own psyche or could rather be interpreted as 'laying the groundwork' to distance himself from his brother.

In that same newspaper interview, Gustav volunteered that he had not seen his brother since December 1984. He further added that his younger brother had teamed up with a group of people from the Bronx and that they were his family now.

Nowhere in the record will you find Gustav Mengel, or for that matter any Mengel family member or confidant with the exception of Phyrween Mengel, express sympathy or act in a conciliatory manner towards the victims of Alex J. Mengel or their families.

25

On March 13, while Mengel was still in Canadian custody and the search for Beverly Capone was being conducted by the state police, the task force began a parallel investigation into Mengel. The investigation was fueled by the suspicious items that were recovered from Mengel's vehicle, the most troubling of which were four wallet-sized photos and one Polaroid of unidentified Caucasian teenage girls.

The next item, a Pennsylvania Tourism Map, seemed innocent at first glance. When investigators examined it closely, they found that a circle had been hand-drawn around the area that denoted Harrisburg. Inside the circle, two areas were marked "X."

WCDPS Detective Mike Henneberry mailed Pennsylvania State Police Homicide Investigator, Corporal Samuel Strauser, a letter regarding Mengel that included his reported practice of frequenting Pennsylvania, along with copies of the map and the pictures of the teenage girls.

On April 17, Henneberry telephoned Strauser to insure that he was in receipt of the items sent. Mysteriously, it was the last time the investigators would speak

Strauser informed Henneberry that although one of the girl's photographs appeared familiar to several troopers in the area, after checking their reports and missing person's flyers, no identification was made.

Strauser's next bit of information was chilling. He reported that the Pennsylvania State Police currently had three unsolved murders in the Harrisburg area, none of which were in the exact locations marked "X" on the map. However, the markings were close enough on the map to be of interest and were being checked out. Strauser further confirmed that the areas demarcated on the map were in the middle of woods or fields.

Strauser also relayed that during the winters of 1982-83 and 1983-84, numerous hunters made complaints about an unknown 'woodsman' in those areas, who was shooting unsafely. Strauser continued that he did interview one hunter, who reported seeing the apparent 'woodsman' up close. Henneberry, in turn said that he would forward a photo of Mengel to Strauser.

In follow-up interviews with Phyrween Mengel, it was learned that Mengel was, for the most part, unemployed during the time frame referenced by Corporal Strauser. According to his wife, Mengel, in 1982, conned a former employer into believing that he was seriously ill and needed an operation. The employer generously continued to pay Mengel his full wages for a year.

Early on in the search for Mengel, his associates, Singh and Mohan, reported that Mengel regularly frequented Pennsylvania, especially the Harrisburg area to hunt and the Langhorne area to attend car auctions and that they had accompanied him many times.

During a later interview with Mohan, shortly before Mengel's demise, Mohan told police that Mengel's lawyers had been around asking questions. Mohan then informed that he was mistaken about taking trips with Mengel to Pennsylvania, having "confused" it with Connecticut.

Following his and his partner's vindication by the grand jury, Fred Grunwald's retort to a reporter's question regarding Mengel was simply, *"Let sleeping dogs lie."*

CASE NUMBER: DD-83-85   DATE OF THIS REPORT: 4/17/85   SHEET NUMBER: 1

On April 17, 1985 (Wednesday) the undersigned telephoned Corporal Samuel Strauser of the Pennsylvania State Police, (717) 234-4051 in reference to this investigation.

Cpl. Strauser informed this writer that he had received the photographs and letter sent on 3/13/85. One of the photographs, (girl with long hair) appeared familiar to several persons in the station but after checking their reports and missing persons flyers, no I.D. could be made on her.

The Pennsylavania State Police have three unsolved murders in the Harrisburg area, none of which were in the exact location marked X on the map. However, the X's were close enough on the map to be of interest and they are being checked out. Cpl. Strauser stated that the places marked are in the middle of woods or fields.

Cpl. Strauser also stated that during the winters of 82-83 and 83-84, numerous hunters made complaints about a "woodsman" living in the area and that he was shooting unsafely. Cpl. Strauser did interview one person who saw the "woodsman." A photograph of Mengel will be sent to Cpl. Strauser.

Det. Michael Henneberry #34

Det. Michael Henneberry #34

DETECTIVE ASSIGNED: SUPERVISING OFFICER:

WESTCHESTER COUNTY DEPARTMENT OF PUBLIC SAFETY
WESTCHESTER COUNTY POLICE
HAWTHORNE, NEW YORK 10532

gc   D82 (10/80)

26

Following Fifteen months of numerous conference calls with Pennsylvania State Police Officials, to obtain information regarding the unsolved homicides, in relation to Mengel's marked map and the girls' pictures referenced during that telephone conversation between Henneberry and Strauser; a call from PSP Corporal George Cronin was received.

Corporal Cronin is a distinguished 30 year veteran of the PSP and is an expert in the investigation of 'cold cases.' A former 'Trooper of the Year,' he holds a Ph.D. in Criminal Justice from Temple University. More interesting, his doctoral dissertation was entitled *Structural detriments of homicides in rural Pennsylvania.*

Corporal Cronin informed that his agency *"has nothing that matches the criteria"* in reference to the pictures of the unidentified teenage girls.

He then advised that he had recently spoken with the now retired Corporal Samuel Strauser, in regards to our questions and that Mr. Strauser stated that he *" 'had no open cases at the time.' "*

The WCDPS Report, Case number DD-83-85 and dated April 17, 1985 that depicts that telephone conversation of more than 30 years ago was emailed to Corporal Cronin for both his and Mr. Strauser's review.

On July 21, Corporal Cronin was contacted in regards to that Freedom of Information Act document. Corporal Cronin stated that after reviewing the document and communicating the information within to Mr. Strauser, That Mr. Strauser stated that he *" 'had no open cases in those areas depicted on the Mengel map.' "*

Corporal Cronin continued that the FOIA document in question … *"is a point of contention with our agency."* Yet, Corporal Cronin did concede that the Mengel map and its markings seemed *"highly coincidental."*

Pennsylvania Tourism Map recovered from Mengel's vehicle.

Pictures of unidentified teenage girls recovered from inside Mengel's vehicle.

27

Antonella Mattina's partial remains were discovered by police on Thanksgiving Day, 1987, in a wooded area off the Taconic State Parkway, in the Westchester suburb of Yorktown. Police responding to a 911 call of illegal deer hunting, recovered a human skull. Days later, an extensive search of those woods, led police to a shallow grave, that contained the rest of Antonella's skeleton.

The state police lab through dental records positively identified the remains as Antonella's. A further examination of the remains, revealed her cause of death - multiple stab injuries to the chest area – just like Beverly Capone. With a new murder case on their plate, the NYSP partnered with the NYPD, the original investigating agency of Antonella's abduction.

As of the writing of this book, no one has been officially implicated in Antonella's abduction or murder. Her case remains officially open by both the NYPD and the NYSP.

Alex Mengel's older brother, Gustav, an electrician, lived at 31-18 Union Street in Flushing at the time of Antonella's disappearance, just six blocks from the Linden Vue Shopping Center; where Antonella was last seen.

In additional interviews with Phyrween Mengel, she reported that Alex visited Gustav at his Flushing home weekly, especially on Sundays. July 16, 1984 was a Monday.

Following his arrest in May 1984, for assaulting his wife, Mengel had few places to turn to for assistance as he habitually failed to pay rent to both family and friends. Even more stressful for Mengel, was never again having access to his longest suffering victim, his wife, Phyrween.

NYPD Detective Anthony J. Lombardi was the lead detective from the Missing Persons Unit assigned to Antonella's case. Detective Lombardi documented several statements from witnesses; among them an eyewitness account of seeing Antonella Mattina with a heavyset white male, approximately 5'8, near the intersection of Willet and Parson Boulevards' on the day she disappeared. This eyewitness is the same person, who called police upon seeing Mengel's newspaper picture on February 25.

Mengel's kidnapping of Beverly Capone along with his brazen

attempt to abduct the thirteen year-old paper delivery girl in broad daylight from a residential street in Skaneateles, at gunpoint, demonstrates his willingness and comfort level in perpetrating such crimes against females of small stature not unlike Antonella.

Additionally, Mengel was not due to see Troy Tranquada at Buffalo University until the next afternoon. What plans did Mengel have for the girl that night? Though Tranquada stated to police that he didn't want to get involved. Exactly how would've Mengel explained the young girl's presence to him? Or would he have already disposed of her?

Retired FBI Supervisory Special Agent Kenneth Lanning, is among the world's leading experts on crimes against children. Lanning, has defined different types of child sexual offenders:

First, there are the true pedophiles − people who prefer sex with children and have them as the subject of their fantasies. Then there are those whose primary sexual urges and fantasies are directed at adults yet may feel too inadequate to pursue the object of their desire and use a child as a substitute.

Lanning classifies these two types of offenders as preferential offenders (true pedophiles) and situational child offenders (the child is more a victim of opportunity then a preferential victim).

Clearly Antonella Mattina was a victim of opportunity, having set out that fateful day for the first time in her young life without the caring eyes of family members upon her.

Lanning also describes the four phases of child abduction for the offender: buildup, abduction, post-abduction, and recovery/release. In the buildup, the subject engages in fantasy that creates some need for sexual activity, although it may not start out child-oriented. He validates and rationalizes his fantasy by talking to others that share or encourage it or by looking at pornographic material that fuels it.

Gustav Mengel was convicted in 2001 of two counts of sexual battery upon a thirteen year-old girl, he spent nine and a half years in a Florida State prison. In 2011, he was arrested again for sexual battery on a child less than twelve years of age, there is no disposition in regards to this case. Both crimes occurred in Broward County, Florida. Gustav Mengel is a Registered Sex Offender in that state.

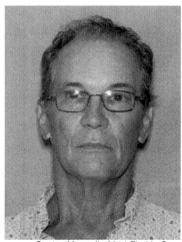

Gustav Mengel's 2014 Florida Sex
Offender Registry photo.

After Mengel's death, Phyrween Mengel revealed to detectives that her husband was so furious that she could not yet have sexual relations with him after their son's birth in 1982 that he attempted to strangle her with a wire and also bit her on the shoulder.

Lanning states that when the offender is ready to carry out the abduction, victim selection is most important. *"Choosing a complete stranger that he can't be linked to is critical to his odds of not getting caught."*

Post-abduction, Lanning explains, is where it really gets stressful for the offender. If the abduction was motivated by sexual fantasy, the subject has to keep the child alive and hidden long enough to carry out the fantasies.

Gustav Mengel's home contained a basement and garage.

Finally, when the pressure gets too high for the abductor, he needs to get rid of the child– dead or alive. The ensuing door to door search by police and massive media coverage of Antonella's abduction was arguably just as intense as NYC's most infamous child abduction case of six year old Etan Patz, on May 25, 1979.

As previously referenced here from Lanning's work, victim selection is vital for the offender. Lanning labels offenders such as these as 'organized offenders' or 'thoughtful offenders.' Another common denominator that these type of offenders share is that they tend to transport their victims over distance. Antonella's remains were located nearly 50 miles away from Flushing.

Mengel's wife and associates stated numerous times to police that a body disposed of by Mengel would not be found as he would … *"put it in a place that you'll never look."* Mengel's extraordinary efforts in secreting Beverly Capone's body, supports these opinions.

Antonella's remains was discovered some 40 months after her abduction, off a parkway, well known by Mengel. A roadway and area that Mengel felt so comfortable with that he attempted his escape there. It was also the same parkway that he travelled on prior to merging onto the Saw Mill River Parkway, the night he assassinated Gary.

The exact area of the find, though scenic, offers no real recreational benefit as it is too close to the noise of a busy parkway and hunting is prohibited; in essence, an ideal spot to conceal a body. Westchester County strictly prohibits hunting with the use of firearms, something that an experienced hunter like Mengel, surely would have known.

Though it was reported that the teenage nephew of a powerful NYC politician, who lived near where Antonella was last seen; immediately retained counsel after being approached by police. Within days, it became clear, to all but one investigator, that the teen was not a viable suspect.

Detective Lombardi discounted the teen as well, believing that Antonella's abduction was stranger perpetrated. Lombardi's belief grew only stronger as time passed and Antonella's whereabouts remained unknown.

All indications are that Tony Lombardi was a first rate cop and skilled detective. He was also the only constant from law-enforcement in the Mattina Family's lives, during the more than three years of not knowing, to the devastating discovery, and through the years that followed. Years that always included timely visits and forthcoming phone calls; that insured there would be justice for Antonella.

With the intent of uncovering a possible work-related link or any other connection between the Mattina family and Gustav Mengel, the Mattina Family was contacted.

On June 16, 2013, Joseph Mattina and his son / Antonella's older brother, Leonard (Leo), graciously met with us in their office. Successful painting contractors in NYC, their operation is impressive with multiple offices and support staff along with teams of skilled painters.

Building this business has clearly been the elder Mattina's life work and the pride and happiness of having his son partner with him is apparent and mutual.

Neither father nor son has any recollection of a Gustav Mengel or any electrical contractor by that name. In fact, their work is and has always been strictly in Manhattan.

With that potential link seemingly disproven, the topic of Antonella's disappearance is broached. Nearly 30 years later, the sadness is still palpable. Joseph Mattina's wife has never forgiven herself for permitting her beloved daughter to carry-out that innocuous errand.

The sense of this close knit family, victimized by soulless predators so many years ago, is as if they feel that they failed Antonella on that day, is truly heartbreaking.

Details of Mengel's death at the hands of police during his escape attempt is shared with the family.

The senior Mattina listens intently then drops a bombshell. He recounts how *"Detective Tony,"* believed to be Detective Anthony J. Lombardi called him about three years ago, long retired and gravely ill. *"He told me the guy, who took Antonella was killed by the police in upstate New York, many years ago."*

NYPD Detective, Second Grade, Anthony J. Lombardi, (Ret.) passed away on May 27, 2010.

Joseph Mattina stated that he and his family want to know why and what exactly happened to his daughter. After more than three decades of suffering, hopefully, the NYPD and the NYSP will not view the evidence against Mengel and the clear investigative link to him as "highly coincidental." Both law enforcement agencies should pursue the answers to those questions, starting with Gustav Mengel.

POSTSCRIPT

Now 30 years later, Gary Stymiloski's legacy is an impressive one. The annual scholarship dinner in his name is hosted by the Westchester County PBA. Over the years, some $450,000 has been raised to provide college scholarships to deserving high school students.

Detective Ken Cody, who was still new to the job when Gary was killed, says the old cliché *"only the good die young"* was true in Gary's case. Pete Rubeo, now retired, also worked with Gary. *"Gary was a natural,"* he says with a smile. Both of these men have been instrumental in keeping the memory of Gary's ultimate sacrifice alive; through their work on the scholarship dinner committee.

Police officer Richard Abramo says Gary's murder was *"crushing."* Abramo partnered with Gary while in narcotics and participated in numerous undercover operations. *"He was the best of the best and from a great family. It was a real shame, a real tragedy."* Abramo said.

Gary Stymiloski's name is inscribed in black granite with the stone figure atop gazing out over the County Center in White Plains. He is the last name listed; there has not been another WCDPS Police Officer murdered in-the-line of duty since. His name also graces a street sign adjacent to WCDPS Headquarters along with an inscribed stone, positioned near the entrance of the building, in a fitting salute to all the fallen WCDPS Officers.

The Stymiloski, Capone and Knapp families mutually agreed years ago not to cooperate with any literary or film representatives, for fear that they may attempt to exploit the violence perpetrated by Mengel; especially as it pertains to Beverly Capone. They have made good on their pact.

The Mattina Family shares a tragic bond with the other families, a grief that no family should experience. As one former classmate of Antonella's observed … *"Antonella's disappearance obviously devastated her family but it also devastated the community."* Antonella's family has found an inner strength that has helped them to persevere and continue their pursuit of justice for Antonella.

Throughout various police jurisdictions in the State of Pennsylvania, there are numerous unsolved missing persons cases and homicides, now considered 'cold cases.' Many of the investigators in these jurisdiction are very interested in learning about Alex J. Mengel.

Currently, a police agency located in the eastern region of the north-central US, is focusing on Mengel, as a suspect in a 'cold case' homicide.

Still other questions remain: Why did the Mengel Family immigrate to South America in the years following WW II? Was Alex Mengel born in

West Germany or South America? And why is there a discrepancy? More intriguing, where, when and how did Alex J. Mengel acquire the skill-set of a killer?

SOURCES

Personal Interviews:
Det. Ken Cody, WCDPS
Cpl. George Cronin, Pennsylvania State Police
D/Sgt. Mike DeRosa, WCDPS (Ret.)
Det. Paul Geiger, WCDPS (Ret.)
Lt. Mike Henneberry, WCDPS (Ret.)
Mr. Joseph Mattina
Mr. Leonard Mattina
Sgt. Tom McGurn, WCDPS (Ret.)
Sgt. Anthony Morizio, WCDPS
Trooper Adam Reed, PIO, Pennsylvania State Police
D/Lt. Jack Roach, Yonkers Police Dept. (Ret.)
Det. Peter Rubeo, WCDPS (Ret.)

Referenced work:
"Child Molesters Who Abduct: Selected Investigative Analysis from Published Articles and Experience" by Kenneth V. Lanning, FBI Supervisory Special Agent (Ret.)
– CAC Consultants- Fredericksburg, VA

Freedom of Information Act documents furnished by:
Westchester County Department of Public Safety

Newspaper Articles:
The Herald Statesman – Yonkers, NY February/March 1985

ABOUT THE AUTHORS

David Paul has over 30 years of experience in the field of Threat Management: having served on active duty with the US Army during the 1980's, as a protection team leader for the CEO of a Fortune 500 Company, and as a Police Officer on Long Island, NY.

Paul has trained with the LAPD's Threat Management Unit and Germany's elite counter-terrorism unit GS-G9.

A student of Russian History and Culture, he speaks, reads and writes the language at an advanced level. These skill allowed him to participate in numerous Russian Organized Crime investigations.

Paul is also a successful screenwriter. *Unearthing a Serial Killer* is his first True Crime book.

He lives in Somers, New York.

dpaul@unearthingaserialkiller.com

Kevin F. McMurray's articles on a variety of subjects have appeared in The New York Times, the Sunday Times, Outside, Men's Journal and others. His books, Deep Descent and Dark Descent, are historical-adventure nonfiction works about notorious shipwrecks.

He also has written five true crime books published by St. Martin's Press.

Kevin lives in Brewster, NY.

kmcmurray@unearthingaserialkiller.com

2015 Gary Stymiloski Scholarship Awards

From left to right – Ken Cody, David Paul, Pete Rubeo and Kevin F. McMurray

MOST WANTED
IN NEW YORK STATE

ALEX J. MENGEL

Wanted by Westchester County Public Safety Office
for the murder of a Police Officer

DOB..1/29/55
Height..5'6"
Weight...200
Hair.................................Sandy Brown
Eyes..Green
Complexion...................................Dark
Race..White
NYSID No..............................5225562R

Mengel is an alien from Dutch Guyana and has a
distinct Indian accent. He is armed and considered to
be extremely dangerous. Citizens should take no action.
If Mengel is located call 1-800-252-4221

32245591R00054

Made in the USA
Middletown, DE
28 May 2016